BRITAIN'S CHANGING TRAIN LIVERIES

BRITAIN'S CHANGING TRAIN LIVERIES

FOUR DECADES OF CHANGE

David Goodyear

AN IMPRINT OF PEN & SWORD BOOKS LTD.
YORKSHIRE - PHILADELPHIA

First published in Great Britain in 2023 by
Pen and Sword Transport
An imprint of
Pen & Sword Books Ltd.
Yorkshire - Philadelphia

Copyright © David Goodyear, 2023

ISBN 978 1 39906 631 0

The right of David Goodyear to be identified as Author of this work has been asserted by him in accordance with the Copyright, Designs and Patents Act 1988.

A CIP catalogue record for this book is available from the British Library.

All rights reserved. No part of this book may be reproduced or transmitted in any form or by any means, electronic or mechanical including photocopying, recording or by any information storage and retrieval system, without permission from the Publisher in writing.

Typeset in 11/14 Palatino
Typeset by SJmagic DESIGN SERVICES, India.

Printed and bound in India by Replika Press Pvt. Ltd.

Pen & Sword Books Ltd incorporates the Imprints of Pen & Sword Books Archaeology, Atlas, Aviation, Battleground, Discovery, Family History, History, Maritime, Military, Naval, Politics, Railways, Select, Transport, True Crime, Fiction, Frontline Books, Leo Cooper, Praetorian Press, Seaforth Publishing, Wharncliffe and White Owl.

For a complete list of Pen & Sword titles please contact

PEN & SWORD BOOKS LIMITED
47 Church Street, Barnsley, South Yorkshire, S70 2AS, England
E-mail: enquiries@pen-and-sword.co.uk
Website: www.pen-and-sword.co.uk

or

PEN AND SWORD BOOKS
1950 Lawrence Rd, Havertown, PA 19083, USA
E-mail: Uspen-and-sword@casematepublishers.com
Website: www.penandswordbooks.com

FOREWORD

Colour adds an essential depth to all that we see. Without it, we would have characterless seasons, a lack of variety in our everyday world – no blue skies, no green grass, no car colour to help identify which car is ours amongst the others, no train liveries – all just a bland grey. No wonder that railway companies in the earliest steam days embellished their locomotives with detailed bright adornments of colour which established pride of ownership and a dedicated sense of striving for the best performance. Distinctive colours applied by the Highland Railway to their 4-6-0 Jones Goods locomotives, and by the London, Brighton and South Coast Railway, whose fine 'Improved Engine Green' impressed with its dark olive green borders lined out with vermilion, black and white, each set exemplary liveries. How could a Midland Railway Class 1000 look any better than in Midland Railway Crimson Lake livery? Great Northern Railway Stirling Singles looked magnificent in full Great Northern Railway (GNR) lined green livery. This trend has in varying interpretation continued ever since, including the dark black of steam locomotives which most companies were later content to parade – for it covered a multitude of sooty smuts and engine muck which would have otherwise looked decidedly untidy. Yet even that black was relieved by outlining and crests or shields. Where steam engines were painted a different colour from black, they were inevitably kept clean in order to sustain the company image.

Below: Hood Bridge, South Devon Railway, Sunday, 24 April 2011: GWR 2251 Class 0-6-0 3205, in Great Western lined green, hauls the 14.17 from Totnes to Buckfastleigh.

The two tone green of the early British Railways diesels earned much admiration, despite it having to compete for attention against the steady withdrawal of steam locomotives which understandably otherwise occupied photographers' interest; the days of BR blue were mundane only because that was the overall colour of trains across the network and any trip to Germany in the late 1990s similarly found a solid wall of red paint on the majority of trains.

Such enterprises as Network SouthEast and the regional colours adopted by Passenger Transport Executives helped to establish a greater variety of colour during the 1980s and 90s by which time privatisation started to raise the appeal of a variety of distinct liveries reflecting ownership and company image. It did backfire on at least one occasion, with the colours forming the branding 'ONE' for the new 'Greater Anglia' franchise launched in April 2004 and which was part of the National Express Group. It seems such a vague, undefined theme simply resulted in a branding which nobody could relate to or understand, apart from a team of designers in an office who were persuaded that such might be a good idea.

Royal Mail red helped link the red mail trains of the 1990s to the product being moved – gone indeed with regret, although still worn by a few Class 325 Postal electric multiple units pacing the West Coast main line between mail facilities. Overall advertising has been seen to improve the image of multiple units such as that of RBS applied to the Heathrow Express Class 332 electric units. Such trains are sleek and lend themselves to this style of livery. The recent variations of ScotRail livery help reinforce a geographical relevance – they are not to be seen south of the Border, apart from at Carlisle. Some Great Western Class 800 IETs had masks applied to acknowledge the need for us to wear face masks whilst travelling by train during the peak of the pandemic – a livery variation with a whole-community relevance.

The purpose of this book is not to provide as many images of British train liveries over the last four decades as possible, but rather to offer a portfolio of how these liveries accompany and complement the different types of trains within the context of their surroundings and era. It is interesting to reflect on the trend towards a more recent revival of some of the popular past-time liveries with rolling stock belonging to the heritage sector and also with examples from within the current and recent fleets of trains serving the national network. I trust that this illustrated survey will simply whet your appetite to seek out further examples in the ever-changing railway scene that expresses this multicoloured rainbow which so brightens our modern and preserved trains. Photographs are arranged in alphabetical order of the relevant illustrated livery to assist readers seeking specific examples of liveries portrayed. Most liveries listed follow the relevant operating company name with a few exceptions, such as the Network Rail New Measurement Train which has changed operators and is currently in the charge of Colas.

My thanks to my wife Valerie for her ongoing patience, support and honest recommendations and to Bernard Mills for assisting with some details of train workings shown in photographs from the earlier decades reviewed in this book, with his truly encyclopaedic knowledge.

ANGLIA

London Liverpool Street, Saturday, 11 September 1999: Class 86/2s, with (left) 86257, ready to depart with the 12.00 service to Norwich, and (right) 86250, both in Anglia Railways livery.

The Anglia Railways livery looked smart and purposeful on these previously West Coast railway line electric locomotives which here intermingled with the intense suburban services which characterised this station. The platform still appears new and surrounding paintwork reflects the fact that the station was given a substantial refurbishment in the late 1980s and which was officially opened by the Queen on 5 December 1991. That refurbishment reinforced the station as very much a cathedral of railway architecture although the embedded grime that preceded it hid much of the Great Eastern Railway glory that fortunately is clearly revived as evident in this photograph.

The Anglia liveried Class 86s saw their final day of passenger service between Norwich and London Liverpool Street on 17 September 2005. They therefore had outlived the younger Class 87s, which were more powerful, on passenger duties.

Ely, Wednesday, 28 May 2008: National Express East Anglia Class 170/2 2-car Turbostar in Anglia Railways livery arrives with the 11.40 ex-Norwich to Cambridge.

The water meadows, marina and River Great Ouse all provide much pleasant countryside walking in this part of East Anglia. In the background is Ely Cathedral, built in the twelfth century, featuring its West tower (215 ft) from the same date, though with its fourteenth century octagonal top section with supporting turrets, and octagonal lantern tower 'the Octagon' (142 ft high) from the same date.

ARC

Merehead Depot approach lines, Saturday, 10 July 1999: Class 59/1 59102 *Village of Chantry* in ARC livery is seen in a light engine movement towards the engine shed. I travelled in the cab of this locomotive within the Merehead site complex during a visit by Plymouth Railway Circle. The JHA wagons seen alongside were owned by Foster Yeoman and built by Orenstein and Koppel of Dortmund, 1989-90.

In many ways, the privately owned fleet of Class 59 locomotives based at Mendip Rail's Merehead depot was trend-setting in that it paved the way for the huge Class 66 fleet deployed by EWS. In daily use, they could *very* reliably haul seriously heavy loads of quarried stone, up to a maximum of 5,000 tonnes, and one was even used to dislodge the two trains which collided at Salisbury Tunnel Junction in late October 2021, becoming fully wedged together. Also see the photographs under the sub-title 'Foster Yeoman and Hanson'.

Little Bedwyn, Monday, 24 July 1995: ARC Class 59/1 59102 *Village of Chantry* passes with mid-afternoon empty west-bound stone hoppers. The flint-stoned fifteenth-century church of St Michaels has a 70 ft high spire.

Here we see 59102 *Village of Chantry* (featured in the previous photograph) passing by the Kennet and Avon canal, which is 87 miles long and links London with the Bristol Channel. It can be seen alongside the Berks and Hants Great Western line for much of the route between Hungerford and Pewsey. It is constantly popular with those who prefer a leisurely journey by narrow boat through this pleasant rural landscape. The frequent IET and stone trains which disturb the quiet will, of course, appeal to any rail enthusiasts amongst the crew.

ARRIVA

Cardiff Queen Street, Saturday, 26 September 2009: Arriva Trains Wales Class 121 Pressed Steel Suburban single railcar 121032/55032 is here operating the 13.12 to Cardiff Bay.

This vintage diesel railcar has seen a wide range of duties indeed. After being based at Tyseley depot for BR passenger service in the West Midlands, it was withdrawn in 1992, after which it was used as a Sandite railcar (No.977842) before acquisition by Pete Waterman for preservation, and it saw use on the East Lancs Railway; it was refurbished and supplied with modern safety equipment such as TPWS (Train Protection and Warning System) and central door locking for use on the Cardiff Queen Street to Cardiff Bay shuttle service in 2006, when in service with Arriva Trains from August that year until withdrawal in March 2013. It was later sold to Chiltern Railways and stored at Aylesbury to supply spares for the two similar railcars used on the Princes Risborough to Aylesbury service. It eventually saw preservation at the Wensleydale Railway for possible use along the Northallerton section of line, and here it remains at present.

Plymouth, Saturday, 26 June 2010: First Great Western Class 150/2 Sprinter units, left: 150278 stabled, right: 150279 which has arrived on the 14.49 from Penzance. Both are based at Exeter at this time, in previous operator Arriva Trains Wales livery and on short term sublease to First Great Western.

  No, this isn't Cardiff Central but it almost could be, with the surrounding office blocks and Arriva Trains Wales livery Sprinter units – not quite the local colours, but that is where the regional liveries contribute an extra dimension to an otherwise familiar local scene. There is probably a map of Cardiff Valley lines to Treherbert and Merthyr Tydfil somewhere on their interiors. Next stop Treforest? Interestingly, of course, there is indeed a link here, for in both the counties of Cornwall and mid-Glamorgan the nearly complete termination of mining has changed the landscape where such industry has become a just memory.

AVANTI WEST COAST

Ansty, Sunday, 30 May 2021: An Avanti West Coast Trains Class 390 Pendolino passes alongside the Oxford canal on its early afternoon northbound service.

After Virgin Trains was taken over by First Group & Trenitalia at the end of 2019, Aura Brand Solutions and Avanti West Coast signed an agreement for the exterior livery branding on the Avanti West Coast Class 390 Pendolino Fleet. The interiors initially remained the same as when these trains operated with Virgin Trains – Avanti has recently undertaken a refurbishment program of the interior and exterior of the units. I consider this livery applied to the power cars to be very attractive although I reserve judgment about the coaches with their part-white section.

Ansty, Sunday, 30 May 2021: The Avanti West Coast Trains Class 390 Pendolino 390119 fully vinyl wrapped 'Pride' train passes alongside the Oxford canal with the 14.16 London Euston to Manchester Piccadilly.

    Avanti West Coast Trains' fully vinyl wrapped 'Pride' train celebrates the diversity of the LGBTQ communities it serves. It reveals a progressive rainbow flag design, a mobile rainbow on rails. Every carriage of this 11-car Pendolino carries a different livery, featuring the colours of the Pride flag – black, brown, light blue, pink and white. It is intended by the train operator to bring to the forefront people of colour, transgender people and those living with or have been lost to HIV/AIDS. It celebrates the need for inclusivity for all. The train most certainly captures the eye and imagination of those whom it passes. It is an interesting purpose of such a livery to make a statement with a specific interpretation, yet which could at the same time appeal to artists, passengers and people of all ages.

BLUEBELL BLUE

Sheffield Park, Bluebell Railway, Tuesday, 4 August 1998: front, South Eastern and Chatham Railway (SECR) Wainwright P Class design 0-6-0T 31323, built 1910, and London, Brighton and South Coast Railway (LBSCR) Class E4 0-6-2T 32473 "Birch Grove," built 1898, arrive with an afternoon train.

The P class of eight small six-coupled tanks were built by Ashford Works between February 1909 and July 1910, being designed for working light branch and push-pull services, replacing the underpowered steam railmotors that had been purchased in 1905/06 for lightly loaded branch services. They were found to be too small for the push pull trains for which they were designed and by 1913 they could be seen all over the system on light shunting work and as shed pilots. In preservation, as an exception to the general rule on the Bluebell Railway, 31323 was repainted in a house style of lined blue livery, with brass number plates and the company crest displayed, a livery based closely on the SECR's Edwardian green livery, and it carried the name *Bluebell* between 1961 and 1998. Four of the eight P class have survived into preservation. Such small locomotives as these, belonging to any of the railway companies of the pre-grouping era, often prove to be of immense appeal to the steam railway fraternity not only because of their diminutive character but also because of their historical longevity and to their survival not as museum pieces but as genuine working locomotives.

BLUEBELL BLACK

Horsted Keynes, Bluebell Railway, Sunday, 24 October 2010: LBSCR Stroudley Class A1x 'Terrier' 0-6-0T 32655 *Stepney* provides local brake van rides.

In the previous photograph we could see *Birch Grove* displaying Stroudley's famous 'Improved Engine Green' gamboge livery, whereas no doubt this black livery makes a reference to that worn by the LBSCR Goods classes, which wore a deep glossy black with two lines of vermilion lining, with lettering which was yellow shaded in red and white. The Class was designed for commuter trains on the heavily congested lines in South and South-East London served by London Bridge and London Victoria. Some of these lines had trackwork of light construction and poor foundations and so were required to be used by lightweight trains. For a locomotive built in 1875, this veteran looks in fine fettle with very few if any leaks of steam emanating from where they shouldn't. (See also page 137).

BR BLACK

Bishops Bridge, South Devon Railway, Sunday, 20 May 2001: Class 04 D2246/11216 shunts a milk wagon and parcels van into the sidings just north of the station.

    A typical rural scene and appropriate train formation for a quiet branch line is recreated here with commendable accuracy. The daily shunting of milk tanks to serve a local cluster of dairy farms reminds us that this was the quickest way to move their fresh perishable products to customers in the large cities. It may have been a time-consuming and costly way of running a train, yet while remote lines closed to passengers in increasing numbers during the 1950s and 1960s, more than a few would continue to see this sort of traffic before faster motorways and larger road tankers could render such time honoured traditions commercially unviable. Our railway heritage can fortunately be recalled in this way on such preservation lines as the South Devon Railway.

Above: Staverton Weir, South Devon Railway, Sunday, 20 May 2001: Class 04 D2246/11216 heads towards Staverton with the 12.13 service from Totnes, hauling an autocoach immediately behind the locomotive.

The 'wasp' stripes may have been a little excessive for this locomotive's occasional use on a quiet preserved rural branch line but these would have been useful in its working in the busy yards near Huddersfield and Barnsley, and additionally at the National Coal Board's Crawley New Yard and Tolworth Coal Concentration depot. Kept clean, its original BR Black livery with cycling lion emblem looks smart and helps establish identity for such an utilitarian shunter.

Opposite above: Hood Bridge, South Devon Railway, Sunday, 24 April 2011: GWR 4500 Class 2-6-2T 5526 is seen hauling the 15.38 Bishops Bridge to Buckfastleigh mixed freight and parcels train.

Nicely reflected in the River Dart, this locomotive clearly displays the British Railways cycling lion emblem. The parcels carriage reminds us that in the days before motorways which now accommodate lengthy parcels lorries, the fastest way to carry mail and parcels was essentially by rail. It is worth recalling that the various main railway companies did much to generate their own perishables traffic along their local branches, and this included grain, potatoes, sugar beet, soft fruit and fish from local ports.

Opposite below: Hood Bridge, South Devon Railway, Sunday, 24 April 2011: Front: GWR 4500 Class 2-6-2T 5526, second: GWR 'Dukedog' 3200 Class 4-4-0 9017, in 1950s BR plain black, haul the 13.22 Totnes to Buckfastleigh.

The 'Duekdog' design was a Collett rebuild using frames of 'Bulldog' class 4-4-0s and boilers and cabs of 'Duke' class 4-4-0 locos. The cycling lion emblem embellishes both locomotives though with that on the 'Dukedog' applied to the tender. The number plate in red helps to break up the plain black. It's an interesting question as to which locomotive is best suited for the dark livery but, kept clean, the black shines out and looks a perfect match, especially when accompanied by this uniform set of coaches.

Ravenglass, Ravenglass and Eskdale Railway, Thursday, 13 August 2009: 2-8-2 *River Esk*. Gauge: 15 inches. 2-8-2 *River Esk* is seen in a light engine run-round movement mid-afternoon.

    Admiring looks from onlookers are fully justified for this gleaming veteran in liveried in Blackberry Black of the LNWR, a close resemblance to BR lined black. The scenic miniature railway wends its way towards the Cumbrian Fells along a route for which *River Esk* was purpose-built, delivered in 1923 from Davey, Paxman & Co of Colchester. The design has provided inspiration for many narrow gauge locomotives that were subsequently built in Britain and Germany between the two world wars. The design by Henry Greenly provided a locomotive capable of working heavy granite trains from Beckfoot Quarry to Murthwaite crushing plant and Ravenglass. It has run thousands of miles over the years since 1952 and offers a commendable level of authenticity within the realm of genuine miniature steam locomotives.

BR LINED BLUE

Waterside, Dartmouth Steam Railway, Sunday, 15 July 2018: GWR 6000 Class 'King' 4-6-0 6023 *King Edward II* passes with the 16.15 Paignton to Kingswear.

Following Nationalisation, experimental liveries appeared in 1948 on some express locomotives, including several which were painted in lined dark blue. The appearance of this blue King on several preserved railways was certainly a highlight of 2017 and all the more welcome on ex-Great Western lines, even if this particular branch line would have hosted less heavy locomotives such as 'Castle' and 'Hall' class locomotives for through London trains from Kingswear. Of course, Kings certainly hauled express passenger trains eastwards from Paignton. 6023 makes a fine sight passing Torbay after a prolonged dry spell judging by the yellow hue of the grass. Fortunately, the picture was not to be compromised by the modern liners which anchored in Torbay during their disuse through the pandemic summers of 2020 and 2021. Just in the distant left can be seen the multicoloured beach huts that characterise several of the local beaches, this one being Goodrington Sands. 6023 *King Edward II* was built in 1930 and worked for most of its life from Newton Abbot and Plymouth Laira sheds.

BR BLUE

Above: Plymouth Laira Depot, Sunday, 15 September 1991: left, Class 42 'Warship' D821 *Greyhound* and right, Class 35 'Hymek' D7018 are on show at the Depot Open Day.

The Southern Region began using Class 42/43 Warships on semi-fast services to the West Country during 1964. The original livery for all D800s was BR green with a light grey waistband and red buffer beams. During the winter of 1990/91, *Greyhound* was repainted into blue livery with yellow warning panels, a very early version of the corporate blue livery adopted by British Railways. Also evident in this scene is the four-character headcode box. Such Open Days were very popular with the general public and were a useful public relations tool.

Opposite above: London Waterloo, Saturday, 22 October 1984: Class 73 73004 in a light engine movement with Class 33 33115 awaiting departure with a mid-morning Exeter service.

The BR Blue era at least benefited from the advantages of uniformity and these two Southern Region locomotives indicate a sense of purpose in their intended duties, even if the litter on the tracks and in the '6 foot' seemed to be tolerated during this period of relative negligence by the railway authorities.

Opposite below: Exeter St Davids, Thursday, 27 October 1983: Right, Class 45 45062 with a southbound freight passes, on the left, Class 45 45074 on a short ECC English China Clays trip freight, mid-afternoon.

The busy freight scene of the BR blue era is reflected here at Exeter, with lower quadrant semaphore signals facilitating the reminiscence of such rail traffic. It is depressing to reflect on the substantial loss of freight to road during the following decades, but there does seem to have been at least some revival as a result of companies such as Tesco being prepared to work with companies like Stobart's to move their containers over long distances. Yet therein lies the problem, for many logistics companies, the attraction of lorries hauling lengthy trailers over shorter distances is worth the time wasted sitting in queues and traffic jams that characterise some parts of the motorway network.

Leicester, Sunday, 21 May 1989: Hertfordshire Rail Tours Inter-City Diesel Day with Class 20s 20228 and 20145 ready to attach to the 12.55 Leicester to London St Pancras Special.

This was a special day of running using freight and out-of-region locomotives on the Midland main line between London St Pancras and Leicester, with some special trains going via Corby. Apart from these two class 20s, Class 33s 33021 and 022, Class 37s 37058 and 066, Class 47 47347, Class 56 56017 and Class 58 58050 took part. Whilst some trains were besieged by the more belligerent enthusiasts, especially those with very rare motive power haulage, other trains were quieter and the day seems to have gone smoothly even if the residents along the quieter sections of line traversed by this unusual fleet of locomotives may have found their quiet Sunday afternoon rather less quiet than they were accustomed to enjoying.

Stoke Cutting, Devonport, Sunday, 1 September 2002: Class 50 50049 leads second in line Class 50 50031, then third 'Western' Class 52 D1015 *Western Champion* and fourth Class 46 46035 along with a support coach, in a light engine movement returning from St Blazey EWS Depot Staff Open Day on the preceding Saturday.

   This is quite a convoy. The Class 50s and *Western Champion* would be destined for their preservation base at the Severn Valley Railway. Class 46 46035 was preserved at 'The Railway Age', Crewe. The immaculate paintwork bears the hallmarks of the care and pride taken in their preserved status and is a tribute to the owners and railways involved in their upkeep. Admittedly they are somewhat easier to keep clean than steam locomotives. It is quite a kaleidoscope of motive power with the locomotives' Maybach, Sulzer and English Electric engines recalling what might be termed 'the diesel era'.

Above: Dawlish, Saturday, 9 July 2011: West Coast Railway's Class 47/4 47804 leads with 'Deltic' Class 55 55022 *Royal Scots Grey* (preserved at the East Lancs Railway) forming Spitfire Railtours' delayed 06.15 Doncaster to Paignton 'The Devonian' which had encountered problems when the Deltic failed at Tiverton Loop.

This classic scene of Dawlish has changed significantly with the recent much needed upgrading of the sea wall. This followed on from a period of more frequent inclement weather, especially the colossal damage to the sea wall in February of 2014 when very strong winds and high seas severely damaged the railway line that runs through Dawlish. The wall between the sea and the railway line was breached, a section of the wall washed away along with 80 metres of track, and damage caused to the platforms at Dawlish railway station. The section of wall being passed by the train, which runs for 360 metres along Marine Parade west of Dawlish station, has been reconstructed with curved panels which deflect waves back out to sea. A further phase of enhancing the sea wall is underway and will provide a high level wider promenade incorporated into a new sea wall alongside renewal of the timber seaward platform. A cool £80 million will then have been invested in this government-funded project.

Opposite above: Edinburgh Waverley, Saturday, 11 September 2021: ROG (Rail Operations Group) Class 47/4 47813 awaits an empty coaching stock move after its journey attached to the rear of the return working of the A1 Steam Locomotive Trust's 'The Aberdonian' hauled by 60163 *Tornado* which has been the highlighted steam locomotive for these excursions in 2021.

The gentle lighting of the complex metallic framework and architecture of the station interior, accompanied by the genuine sound of the Class 47 Sulzer engine ticking away, attached to its traditional liveried rake of carriages, provides a genuine recollection of night trains during the BR blue diesel era, even if the face masks worn by some onlookers alert us to the fact that this is post-Covid Britain.

Below: Tavistock Junction, Friday, 1 February 1991: Class 08 08576 is occupied with shunting duties, soon to be passed by Class 47/4 47801 working the 12.13 Plymouth to Manchester Piccadilly.

Although downsized since this picture was taken, Tavistock Junction still provides a service to Colas. The rake of Railfreight 'Speedlink' vans stabled on the right is of particular interest as they would soon become redundant. They were branded with a white BR logo alongside the 'Railfreight' wording on a red stripe background at the top and the ends were painted red. The remainder of the van was grey. 'Speedlink' provided a traditional freight distribution service in which individual wagons from various distribution centres (both railway and privately owned) and individual factory sidings were shunted into a single train at Speedlink regional centres. After arriving at their destined regional centre, the wagons would be then sorted and delivered to their separate ultimate destinations. This service benefited from a slick process not shared by existing freights. Unfortunately, although established to be a profitable venture for BR, Speedlink made considerable losses each year, which saw its total withdrawal in 1991.

Opposite above: Bewdley Tunnel, Severn Valley Railway, Thursday, 18 May 2017: Class 45 45041 hauls the 14.35 Kidderminster to Bridgnorth as it emerges past early autumnal colours in the surrounding trees and bushes.

This could easily be a location in the Peak District or Pennines, or even parts of the Settle and Carlisle railway. Such territory was familiar to these hard working locomotives tackling the gradients which enabled enthusiasts to gain a fine impression of their inherent power, often hauling lengthy passenger trains over those scenic lines. They conveyed a sense of purpose and reliability, and the BR blue livery certainly suited them. Often seen weathered during their everyday duties, it all conveyed a sense of a machine amidst nature's wild landscapes.

Opposite below: Near Foley Park, Severn Valley Railway, Thursday, 18 May 2017: Class 50 50008 *Thunderer* hauls the 12.08 Bridgnorth to Kidderminster up the grade towards Bewdley Tunnel.

The InterCity rake of carriages appears to be an appropriate accompaniment for a locomotive which would have worked such stock when plying the Western Region main line to and from the West Country. It would need to be kept clean if it was to remain presentable, and carriage washers had a tendency to wear the paintwork – but regular cleaning paid dividends in terms of the resulting smart business-like aura conveyed by a complete set as on show here. The Class 50 will enjoy the opportunity to stretch its wings along the lengthy preservation railway and especially on this climb at 1 in 100 at its steepest.

Below: Paignton, Dartmouth Steam Railway, Saturday, 28 August 2021: Class 03 03371 shunts empty coaching stock.

The Class 03 locomotives, one of British Rail's most successful 0-6-0 diesel-mechanical shunters, which could be found working on London Midland and Eastern Region metals, have proved especially popular in preservation with 54 locomotives represented across the UK at a recent count. Versatile and lightweight, in their role with British Railways their short wheelbase and relatively low weight enabled them to work where other engines, like Class 08 shunters, were more restricted. Now they fulfil a key role such as here in moving stock around without the need for burning valuable coal in steam locomotives which otherwise need that expensive fuel for their dedicated passenger duties. The 'Wasp' stripes would have proved useful when working in railway yards and alongside roads at docks such as at Boston and Bidston.

Above: Lee Moor Crossing near Plym Bridge, Plym Valley Railway, Sunday, 20 October 2019: Sentinel 10077 with a brake van heads past early autumn colours en route to Marsh Mills.

This locomotive spent its industrial working days in Yorkshire. Built by Rolls-Royce, Shrewsbury in 1961, it was employed at Raisby Tarmac Quarry, Coxhoe, County Durham. In preservation it has spent time at a small number of locations, and in more recent times has been purchased privately and moved to the Plym Valley Railway for restoration. It has been used for brake van rides and for moving maintenance trains along the branch, with its 230hp providing more power than that supplied by the Class 03 previously featured. In quasi-BR blue and with a BR double arrow emblem, it qualifies herein as an unusual representative of that livery.

Opposite above: Watchet, West Somerset Railway, Saturday, 25 September 1999: 'Western' Class 52 D1010 *Western Campaigner* leads 'Warship 'Class 42 D832 *Onslaught* with the 14.50 Minehead to Bishops Lydeard.

It would be marvellous to hear the combined sound of these two diesel hydraulics echoing through the cutting as they accelerate away from the picturesque harbour of Watchet. It would also be an interesting exercise to find out how many such combinations occurred in real practise. As both classes were allocated to BR Western Region, such would have certainly been a possibility, even if a rarity. The small yellow warning panel on *Western Campaigner* can be considered to distinguish this version of BR blue as opposed to the full yellow end of the 'Warship.'

Opposite below: Blue Anchor, West Somerset Railway, Sunday, 1 October 1995: Class 42 'Warship' D832 *Onslaught* arrives with a late afternoon parcels train from Bishops Lydeard.

A reflective picture which captures a typical branch parcels service amidst a late 1960s scene with the characterful station adorned by canopies with its milk churns placed on a trolley ready to load on to the next Up service. The BR blue with full yellow ends did not appeal with some of the diesel classes but it looks much at home here. The station is deserted – a reminder that services would too often be very limited on such branch lines, and the subsequent lack of use then used to justify closure of these arteries which fed in to the main line network. It is fortunate that we are seeing a reversal of such policies with prime examples being the partial reopening of the Scottish 'Borders' line from Edinburgh to Galashiels and Tweedbank and the more recent reopening of the Okehampton branch to Exeter.

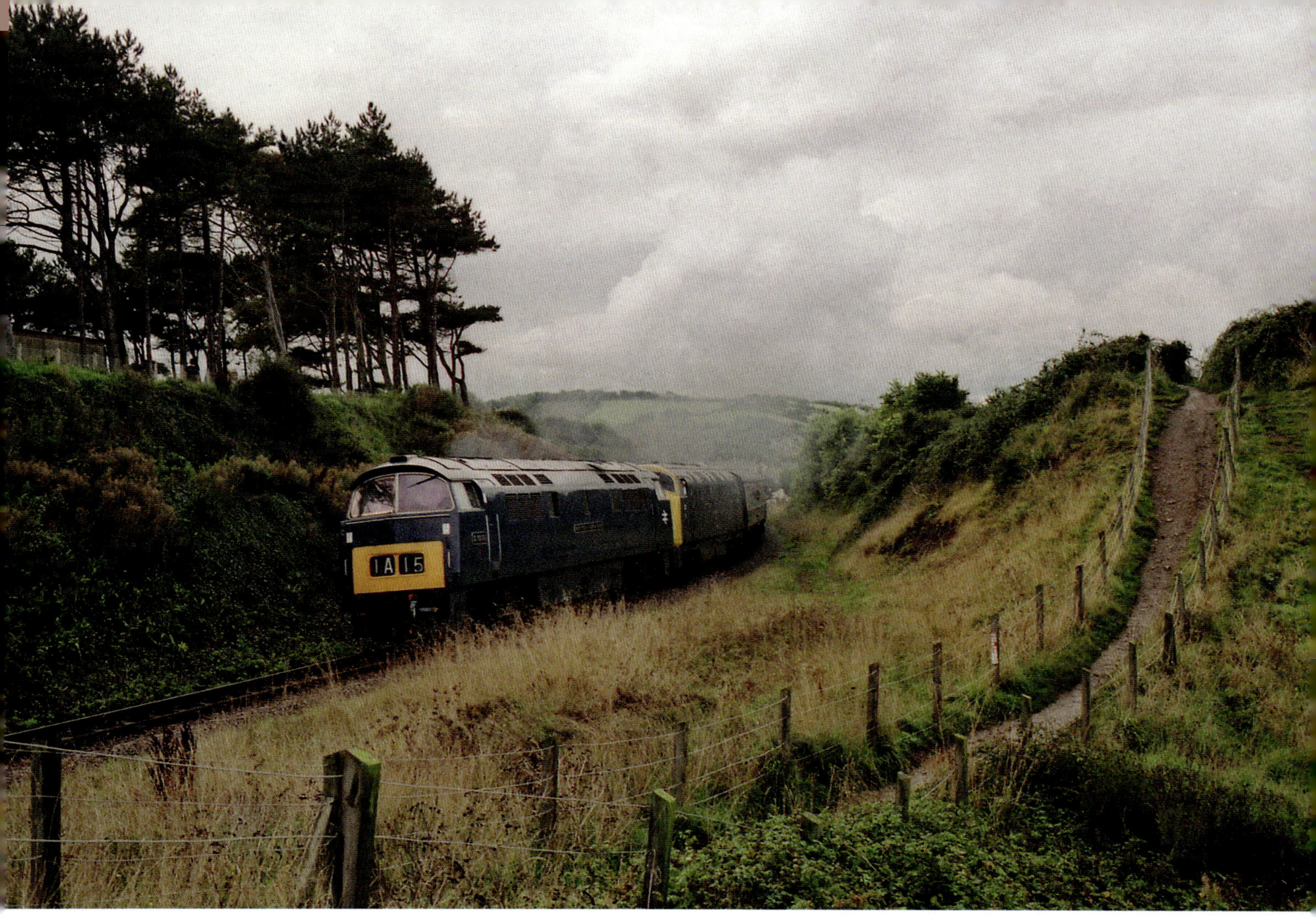
1A15

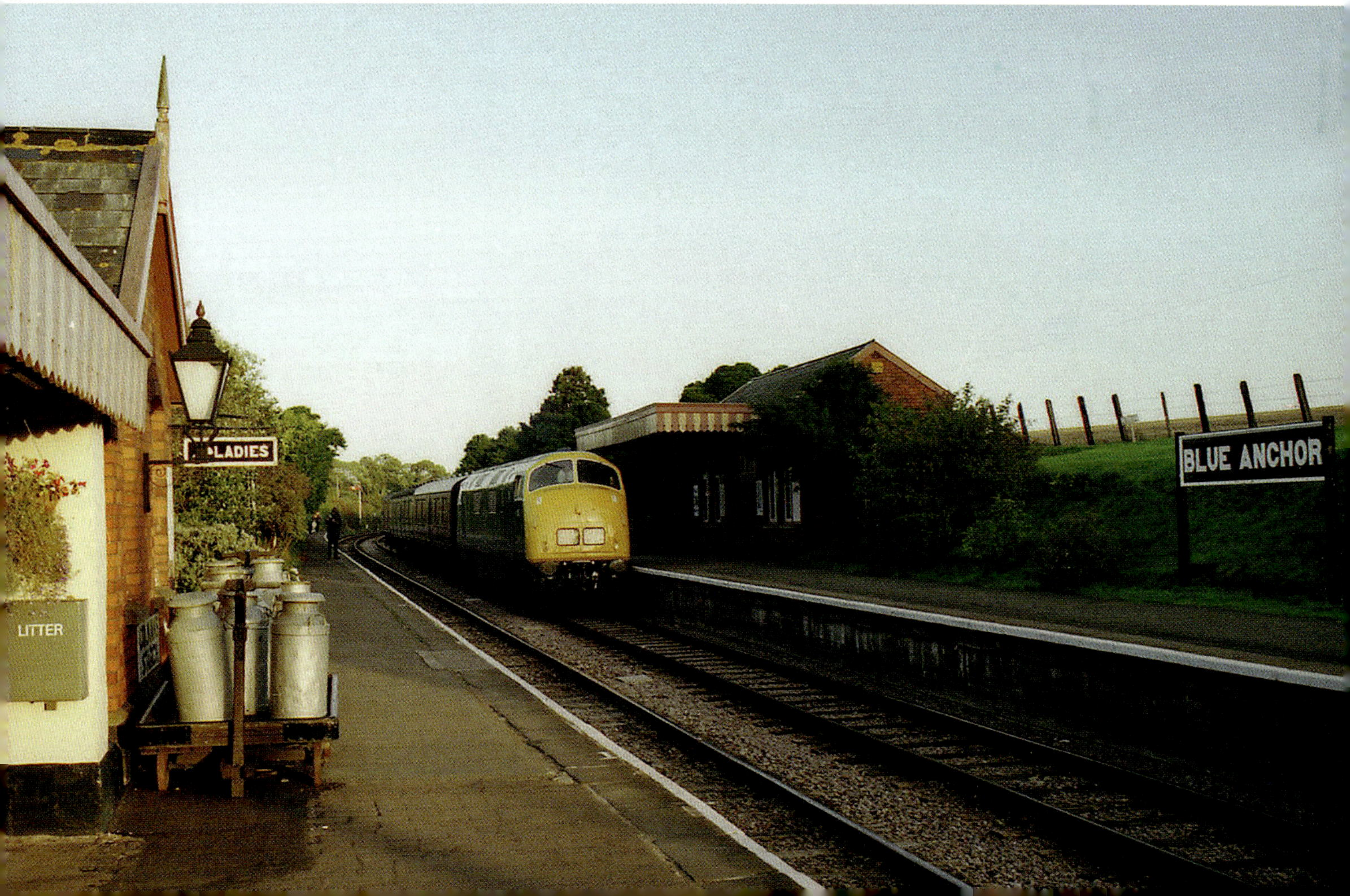
LADIES
BLUE ANCHOR
LITTER

Opposite above: Buckfastleigh, South Devon Railway, Monday, 22 April 2019: Class 25 D7535/25185 and Class 33 33002 are stabled at the Ashburton end of the station.

An opportunity is here provided to compare the two standard BR green and blue liveries which adorned diesel traction in the 1970s. The two locomotives were deployed with six-carriage trains in tow reflecting the busy services during the Whit half-term week of 2021. The Class 33, and later in the season the Class 25, was also booked for the final service of each weekday, on the South Devon Railway during the summer peak. It was evident that local diesel enthusiasts made the effort to ride behind the locomotives, and it is a pleasing trend of some of the larger preserved railways, notably the Severn Valley Railway, to timetable a main line diesel from their home fleet for their off-peak services.

Opposite below: Toddington, Gloucestershire Warwickshire Steam Railway, Sunday, 21 October 2018: Pressed Steel Class 117 three-car diesel multiple unit W51405, W59510, W51360 or 51372 arrives with a mid-afternoon shuttle from Winchcombe carrying visitors attending the food and drink local produce fair.

With the sort of mixed livery that occurred during the transition period from BR green to BR blue during the late 1960s and early 1970s, these three-car units spent most of their lives on the commuter services out of London Paddington, Plymouth and Cardiff. The early autumn colours and sunshine help to set the scene which could easily be one of the rural stations served by these units which provided a much superior ride than the Pacers which succeeded them.

Below: Foley Park, Severn Valley Railway, Thursday, 18 May 2017: Class 55 Deltic 55022 *Royal Scots Grey* ascends the grade towards Bewdley Tunnel with the 13.42 Bridgnorth to Kidderminster.

Here is a detail difference displayed by *Royal Scots Grey* operating as 55018 *Ballymoss* and which the green liveried Deltics also carried – the cab windscreen and side window surrounds were picked out in white on some of the Deltics when in service, mainly those based at Finsbury Park. It is a refinement which helps them looks distinguished and it further reinforced the fact that the Deltics were indeed a class set apart from the more humble classes of traction, with their higher power output, dedication to east coast main line expresses and their characteristic hum. The sound of the Napier Deltic engines working hard will no doubt please the enthusiasts on board this train – I recall (after returning from job interviews) listening to these locomotives during the early 1980s accelerating through Copenhagen tunnel shortly after leaving London King's Cross, and a pleasant deafening of the ear drums was more than a worthy tribute to these powerful steeds. Even the yellow gorse pays tribute to the cab's yellow front as it echoes a matching colour almost to perfection.

BR BLUE LARGE LOGO

Above: Teignmouth Sea Wall, Friday, 4 August 1989: Class 50 50008 *Thunderer* on a civil engineers train from Exeter Riverside to Tavistock Junction.

In an earlier guise than that seen at the Severn Valley Railway, and in BR blue large logo livery, this Class 50 emerges from Parsons Tunnel in familiar territory for these locomotives. It is a reminder that these main line passenger locomotives were called on to operate less demanding but ever important duties such as portrayed here. The red Permian sands' colouration is a striking feature of the South Devon coastline at Dawlish and Teignmouth. Ancient winds piled up these sands upon what was a gravelly desert floor and the result are these fossilised sand dunes. Wind erosion on these cliffs has produced some striking patterns and forms in the exposed sand.

Opposite above: Truro, Wednesday, 25 April 1984: Class 50 50029 *Renown* heads an eastbound parcels, early afternoon.

This Class 50 has been preserved, although it is very unlikely to see use on this sort of lengthy parcels train again. Surely most of these vans will have seen the cutter's torch. Admittedly, now that much that would have been posted can be sent as attached files to emails and so forth, it could be argued that there is less demand to send parcels and yet the Amazon revolution has seen fleets of dedicated vans now delivering daily parcels in vast quantities that would never have been predicted at the time of this photograph. Still, it's a hefty load that will tax the Class 50 as it climbs the rolling gradients of the Cornish hills and tackles the steep gradients of the South Devon main line.

Below: Plympton, Saturday, 24 September 1983: Class 50 50040 *Leviathan* with a nine-carriage train forming the 10.35 Newquay to London Paddington, passing the site of the old Goods Yard just after midday.

An impressive image is here provided by a uniform BR blue locomotive and carriage set, and consequently it can be argued that this livery was aesthetically interesting; it was just the case that everything was painted in the same colour scheme and therefore it lost its appeal. 'Variety is the spice of life' is a phrase often used, and we can now reflect back on how well certain liveries applied to different types of rail traffic. There are still through workings to Newquay by IETs and in previous times even nine-carriage HSTs climbed their way along the curvaceous charms of the Luxulyan valley and past the branch's wayside stations that saw very little service on Summer Saturdays because of the priority given to the visiting main line trains. This train would have looked equally impressive along the Newquay branch and would have provided much entertainment to the haulage enthusiasts on board, no doubt to be found as close to the locomotive as they could get.

Above: Hemerdon Summit, Friday, 9 October 1992: Class 47/4 front: 47580 *County of Essex* in BR blue large logo livery, second 47471 *Norman Tunna G.C.* in InterCity livery hauling the 16.45 Plymouth to York parcels which was regularly double-headed at the time.

Double-headed trains are rarely a feature in today's rail traffic, thanks to much increased power and adhesion of newer locomotives' engines, but in previous times these provided necessary back-up for mail and parcels trains, and for some of the Class 50 hauled Up-Sleeper overnight trains within Cornwall. These provided interesting photographic opportunities when locomotives bestowed with differing liveries happened to be paired. Both are clearly working hard here to clear the top of the steep incline; there is some dispute whether the Class 800 IETs can climb Hemerdon as quickly as their forerunner HSTs.

Opposite above: Devonport, Saturday, 29 June 2002: Class 47/4 47847 *Railway World Magazine* in BR blue large logo livery accelerates with the 10.15 Manchester Piccadilly to Penzance.

The Class 47s were somewhat derided during their years of service with British Rail, partly because they superseded the steam locomotives which had inspired awe and wonder for generations of train enthusiasts and also because they constituted a much larger fleet than the other classes (512 in total) which, by virtue of being built in smaller batches, tended to be viewed as having more character. Certainly, if there were only twenty-two of them as in the case of the Deltics, they would surely have commanded more respect. As time has passed, however, those that remain in use with private operators or in preservation have increased in their appeal and probably have now earned their deserved respect.

Below: Polbathic Bridge near St Germans, Friday, 25 September 2020: Class 47/4 47593 *Galloway Princess* leads class 47/4 47805 with the 'Cornish Riviera Statesman' 06.08 York to Penzance.

Thanks to Locomotive Services Ltd., these Class 47s amply demonstrate the point made in the previous photograph about the increased appeal of the class, especially when adorned with genuinely retrospective liveries, and how smart they look as they climb up from St Germans to Trerulefoot with the pleasant east Cornwall landscape and with Dartmoor in the background. The front four carriages in Pullman livery add further variety of colour and the trees make their own contribution as they are just starting to acquire their autumnal tints.

Above: Coombe by Saltash viaduct, Saturday, 3 July 2021: Class 47/4 47593 *Galloway Princess* leads class 47/4 47853 with the 'Cornish Riviera Statesman' 04.50 Derby to Penzance.

This view of the 'Cornish Riviera Statesman' crossing the seven span viaduct which traverses an inlet off the River Tamar Estuary just west of Saltash provides an interesting opportunity to compare the two blue liveries which characterised the BR blue era. These Statesman charters were one of the few reliable excursions to grace the lines into Cornwall during the periods of time during 2020 and 2021 when post-pandemic lock-down was cautiously eased. Their appearance was very much appreciated by the local enthusiasts and they seem to have attracted fine weather during both occasions – a just reward for patient photographers and for equally resilient passengers on board.

Opposite below: Cockwood Harbour, Saturday, 26 September 2020: Class 47/4 47593 *Galloway Princess* leads the 'Torbay Riviera Statesman' 16.23 Kingswear to Penzance via Exeter.

The lucky punters aboard this train must have truly enjoyed their late afternoon trip in perfect lighting along the scenic coastline of the Exe estuary captured on camera at this ever-popular photo-location. The Class 47, operated by Locomotive Services Ltd, carries the Scotty Dog emblem which reminds us that it was once based at Eastfield depot, Glasgow and was named *Galloway Princess* at Stranraer station after the flagship of Sealink's Stranraer-Larne service, to stress the links between BR and Sealink and the relaunch of the Glasgow to Stranraer/Larne to Belfast route.

BR BLUE AND GREY

Above: Eggesford, Thursday, 2 August 1990: Class 101 Metro Cammell dmu departs with the 13.01 Barnstaple to Exeter St Davids.

Here a diesel multiple unit displays standard coaching stock livery of BR blue with light grey window bands. The train may be ordinary and everyday, for its era, but the station is a fine piece of railway architecture. Built in a Tudor Gothic style for the London and South Western Railway in 1850, Eggesford Station originally consisted of one building which incorporated the station master's residence as well as the ticket office, parcel store, waiting room and toilets. Noteworthy is the bay window overlooking the platform, part of the ladies' waiting room. The station is somewhat remote with the nearest large village of Chulmleigh being over two miles away and inevitably requiring the residents to take a taxi or be given a lift by car. If heading towards Barnstaple, passengers will have time to admire this marvellous rural station building while awaiting the arrival of the Up train before accessing the single line for their onward journey.

BR GOLDEN OCHRE

Bridgnorth, Severn Valley Railway, Saturday, 9 October 2021: Class 14 D9551 is stabled outside the locomotive shed.

What might have been? The livery suits the locomotive and matches the colour of the nearby wagons, although D9551 carries a non-original 'golden ochre' livery, which was uniquely an experimental livery which in BR days only adorned Western locomotive D1015 *Western Champion*. The colour scheme would have been appropriate for the duties performed by this class, working trip movements between local yards and short-distance freight trains. Preservation allows such possible liveries to be explored and adds an extra dimension of interest to the traditional colours of blue and green worn by these locomotives in their daily duties with British Railways and later, for this locomotive, with British Steel at Corby Steelworks.

BR GREEN

Clapham Junction, Wednesday, 11 April 2001: Class 33/2 D6593/33208, in BR green livery, awaits duties alongside Class 159 159004 in Network SouthEast livery.

This Class 33 was based at the Mid Hants Railway and owned by 71A Locomotives at the time of this photograph. The contrast in colour between this heritage locomotive and the surrounding multiple units could not be greater, with the Network SouthEast bright livery compared to the green locomotive with its white cab wrap-around white and small yellow warning panel. The first Class 33 to be painted in this scheme was D6530 in June 1962. 33208 had been withdrawn from service with BR in February 1997 when based at Stewarts Lane Depot. I can find no record of its purpose at Clapham Junction on this occasion.

Above: Buckfastleigh, South Devon Railway, Sunday, 11 May 2003: Class 33 33110 in BR green livery departs over Mardle Bridge with the 14.00 milk train, bound for Bishops Bridge sidings.

The white cab and white stripe along the body side helped relieve the green on these locomotives. Many Class 33s remained in green livery well into the mid-1960s, with several bearing the livery until their repaint into BR blue as late as 1968. It could be a typical working along a rural line from the 1960s, collecting the milk tanks for their swift delivery to the cities and towns for tomorrow's breakfast cereal and cups of tea. There is some evidence of track replacement in the foreground, a reminder that permanent way maintenance is an ongoing requirement in the heritage sector as much as with the national network and must be managed around the times that the railway is open for running scheduled trains.

Opposite below: Totnes Riverside, South Devon Railway, Wednesday, 11 April 2019: Class 33/0 D6501/33002 waits to run around its coaching stock before its return on the final train of the day, to Buckfastleigh.

Looking rather like a late summer's afternoon rather than springtime, this photograph pays tribute to the standard of restoration in preservation given to the Class 33s eighteen years exactly after the previous photograph. The guard will have enjoyed a trip in the brake/compartment coach immediately behind the locomotive and awaits pulling the levers at the adjacent Riverside Ground Frame, which is released from Ashburton Junction signal box and thus enables the loco to traverse the junction seen to the right (with the Great Western main line in the background).

Below: Bridgnorth, Severn Valley Railway, Saturday, 14 October 1989: Class 45 D100 *Sherwood Forester* prepares for the day's duties.

If there is any doubt that BR green accompanied by a split headcode, small yellow warning panel, white sole bar and grey roof attained the pinnacle of that livery, here is an exemplar that deserves to turn as many heads as any pristine express steam locomotive. The nameplate and BR Roundel add further authenticity and help recall the heyday of these locomotives' work on the Midland main line. They were truly a magnificent sight and established a well-deserved reputation for reliability and efficiency in the early days of BR transition from steam to diesel. Interestingly, although heavy locomotives, the 2,500 hp 'Peaks' proved equal to the 'Westerns' when considering their performance over a wide speed range, and also proved capable of matching the Class 47s in their mixed duties. The yellow panel recalls the fact that the introduction of such was in response to the steadily increasing use of quieter diesel and electric locomotives in the early 1960s which, compared to the hiss and noise of a hard working steam engine, posed an increased risk to trackworkers' lack of awareness of approaching trains.

Above: Royal Albert Bridge, Saturday, 25 June 2011: Class 31s, front Class 31/1 31190 as 5613, in BR green (with white stripe) and second Class 31/6 31601 in DCR (Devon and Cornwall Railway) dark green livery, crossing into Devon with Pathfinder Tours' return excursion 'The Mazey Day Cornishman' from Penzance to Tame Bridge Parkway. The front two carriages are from the Riviera coaching set.

Both locomotives at this time belonged to British American Railway Services which had acquired Hanson Traction, a spot-hire company which owned 31190, during 2010. Devon and Cornwall Railway had been involved with establishing a potential service from Okehampton to Exeter, although this only came to fruition when Network Rail redeveloped the line for a two-hourly service which started in November 2021, although that was provided by Great Western Railway using paired Class 150s. These very rare visitors to Cornwall catch the midsummer's evening light nicely, for the encroaching sea mist has lifted enough to afford the passengers their grandstand view over the River Tamar from the famed bridge. 31601 received a new livery of all over grey during the spring of 2015 and was named *Devon Diesel Society* which is the diesel preservation group based at the South Devon Railway.

Opposite below: Venton, Saturday, 30 October 2021: Class 40 locomotives, front D213/40013 *Andania*, second D345/40145, with a full InterCity livery Mk3 and Mk2 Statesman coaching set, ascend the grade towards Marley tunnel forming the Locomotive Services operated 06.25 Preston to Plymouth 'The Devonian Double'.

This scene really is the paragon of Class 40s in preservation – the BR Dark Brunswick green livery applied to perfection and with 40013 bearing the Cunard Lines nameplate; the sound has to be imagined but it lived up to expectations. Even the frost grilles (covering slatted air intakes) are immaculately polished. I recall seeing lines of these locomotives stabled at Crewe over weekends during the early 1970s, duly noting the numbers carefully to ensure that as many as could be were underlined in my Ian Allan *Motive Power* book. At this time, they were booked for some TransPennine services from Liverpool Lime Street to York and Scarborough and I recall their distinctive whistle resounding especially off the various tunnel walls through which they passed en route. By then, the majority were in blue, although 40106 became a celebrity for, although repainted into blue and yellow as late as September 1978, shortly afterwards it was decided to repaint the loco in Dark Brunswick green with full yellow ends. 40106 then became a popular locomotive servicing railtours and special passenger workings for several years more.

Below: Royal Albert Bridge, Tuesday, 6 April 2021: Class 37/5 D6851/37667 in BR green livery heads the 'West Wales and West of England' Locomotive Services Limited private charter train 09.01 from Truro to Plymouth.

Passengers on board this special train will undoubtedly have admired the immaculate paintwork bestowed on the Class 37 as they boarded and can now enjoy the fine views afforded from the Royal Albert Bridge, here looking towards Cornwall and the River Tamar's wide stretch of waters where they meet the River Tavy. The line to Bere Ferrers and Gunnislake passes below, having once carried LSWR traffic from Plymouth to Tavistock, Okehampton and Exeter Central for onward travel to London Waterloo. The itinerary for the passengers on this fine spring day involved further scenic splendours with an afternoon trip along the Dartmouth Steam Railway via Paignton.

Above: Corfe Common, Swanage Railway, Sunday, 12 September 2010: SR 4-6-2 West Country Pacific 34028 *Eddystone*, with the 14.30 Norden to Swanage.

Eddystone's BR Brunswick green livery stands out particularly well both against the Southern green coaches and the late summer green countryside of Corfe Common, and the red berries salute the bright red nameplate. Rebuilt in 1958, this locomotive provided service until withdrawal in April 1964. Many of the rebuilt West Country Pacific locomotives were withdrawn soon after their rebuilding, and the first of these was 34028 *Eddystone*. Once fully restored by Southern Locomotives in 2003, it consequently returned to its role hauling passenger trains on the Swanage Railway for ten years before being withdrawn in 2014 for a major overhaul. After three years of dedicated work on the boiler and a new tender tank, it was proudly returned to working service.

Opposite above and opposite below: Corfe Castle, Swanage Railway, Sunday, 12 September 2010: SR 4-6-2 Battle of Britain Pacific 34070 *Manston* at the rear of the 16.30 Norden to Swanage.

Lined BR green looks wonderful in such immaculate paintwork on this superbly restored steam engine, the last locomotive to be built by the Southern Railway before Nationalisation on 1 January 1948. Early in its career, *Manston* proudly hauled services on the main lines to the Kent ports at Folkestone and Dover, and was used on the Continental boat trains including the Night Ferry. Later it stretched its legs on the Southern Railway's enchanting routes in Devon and North Cornwall as well as on the main line between Exeter and Salisbury.

34070 *Manston* returned to service on the Swanage Railway in 2008 when it double headed a service train with 34028 *Eddystone*, its compatriot illustrated in the previous photograph. In preservation it offers a chance to see and enjoy haulage behind a fully restored representative of the Battle of Britain Class in its original Bulleid condition.

Above: Buckfastleigh, Monday, 22 April 2019: Great Western 6400 Class 0-6-0PT 6412 stabled with GWR autocoach 233.

Built at Swindon in 1934, this pannier tank looks particularly smart in its BR lined Brunswick green livery, and well matched with the GWR chocolate and cream borne by the autocoach. With 6412 fitted for push/pull services, in this formation the pair would have facilitated a quick turn-around at termini on short branches where running a tender locomotive would use precious time in running around its train and necessitate a run-around loop. An additional facility with which the autocoach was equipped were the unfolding steps operated by a handle in the vestibule; this was used at low platform basic halts. 6412 enjoys life in preservation at the South Devon Railway and its use along such a branch line is entirely authentic.

Opposite above: Venton, Friday, 1 October 2021: Stanier Class 6P 'Jubilee' 4-6-0 45596 *Bahamas* pilots London and North Eastern Railway (LNER) Class B1 4-6-0 61306 *Mayflower* on the 11.00 Plymouth to London Victoria 'Mayflower to Devon and Cornwall' tour operated by Steam Dreams.

Here is a rare chance to compare two contemporary green liveries that would have been worn by these locomotives during the same post-nationalisation era. *Mayflower* was built in 1948 by the North British Locomotive Company in Glasgow but was delivered post-nationalisation and acquired the number 61306 from British Railways. Looking authentic in the early British Railways apple green livery originally given when delivered in 1948, *Mayflower* returned to full main line operation in early 2019 after an extensive overhaul. Coincidentally, February 2019 saw the first main line run of LMS Stanier Class 6P Jubilee 4-6-0 No 45596 *Bahamas* for 35 years. It enjoyed a series of railtours during 2021, and here is seen as such proudly wearing its Brunswick green BR livery.

Below: Buckfastleigh, South Devon Railway, Wednesday, 29 August 2019: Gloucester RCW diesel railcar Class 122 W55000 (DMBS), preserved at the South Devon Railway, stabled.

This 1958-built diesel railcar, originally fitted with AEC engines and equipment later replaced with Leyland 6/80 150hp engines, spent its time working in the southwest and West Midlands. While at the South Devon Railway, it has been used for off-peak trains at the end of the day, or as a shuttle for special events. It is popular with passengers and drivers, although out of service at the time of writing. This type of diesel unit would have looked especially at home on the Cornish and South Devon branches. The standard of this railcar's restoration is exemplary in both its authenticity and perfect colour match.

Above: Caddaford Curve, South Devon Railway, Sunday, 4 April 2010: Gloucester RCW diesel railcar Class 122 W55000 passes alongside the River Dart with the 13.55 Buckfastleigh to Staverton.

Here is a chance to compare the BR green with whiskers livery applied to the same train as in the previous photograph; it could be a contender for the best livery worn by these units, and the swirl of the cream whisker adds to a sense of movement which, while lacking haste, reflects the lower speeds that often applied to branch lines along which speed was less important than providing a decent service to the local communities within the rural areas of Britain.

Opposite above: Consall Forge, Churnet Valley Railway, Sunday, 16 August 2009: BRCW Class 104 dmu 50455/50517, preserved at the Churnet Valley Railway, crosses the Caldon Canal with the 12.52 Cheddleton to Froghall.

Not to be overlooked is the BR green with whiskers that adorned diesel multiple units in the 1960s. The white cab roof dome and lighter grey carriage roof tended to be a characteristic of the Manchester Piccadilly to Buxton route on which these Class 104s operated. They gave a lively if firm ride and afforded a fine view of the line from seats immediately behind the front and back cabs. The cream lining gave further relief to the overall green, as well as the two-character headcode. It was a stylish design as well as meeting a purpose of providing a warning.

Below: Buckfastleigh, South Devon Railway, Sunday, 11 May 2003: Derby Suburban Quad Class 127 dmu 51592/51604 arrives with the 13.40 from Staverton.

With two Rolls-Royce C8 engines giving 476 hp (355 kW) per power car, these were powerful diesel units which were dedicated to serving the commuters along the London St. Pancras to Bedford route. Their hydraulic transmission set them apart from other dmus. They worked hard on schedules with intense diagrams, and all those slam doors to each seating bay must have been a bit of a challenge to the guards dispatching their train from each station, as they would need to see all doors were properly closed. Ten vehicles of this class were preserved at the time of this photograph but only eight now survive. Such diesel units as these acted as workhorses connecting local communities along branch and main line routes but were taken for granted by photographers and rail enthusiasts who preferred locomotives heading rakes of carriages.

Above: Washford, West Somerset Railway, Sunday, 1 October 1995: Class D120/45108 arrives with the 16.45 Bishops Lydeard to Minehead.

With a little imagination and wishful reminiscence, we could be looking at a Saturday's only 'Holiday Makers' daytime excursion train to Minehead, or even a special train bound for Butlin's holiday camp. We should not forget that the railways, with their improved infrastructure and cheap travel options, had created the day tripper, forever changing the landscape of seaside towns across the United Kingdom. The railway companies actually enhanced such destinations by providing easy and affordable ways of reaching the coasts from any inland conurbations. The 'Wakes weeks', when woollen mills and factories in Lancashire and Yorkshire closed for their annual break, saw huge numbers of passengers travel to Blackpool for a week's stay during the summer peak, and seaside towns welcomed day visitors in their droves. Lancashire's railway system, which developed primarily to serve the needs of the county's thriving industries, had the added advantage of opening up hitherto inaccessible areas of country and seaside to day trippers.

Railway companies were quick to respond with organised excursions, aimed directly at workers celebrating their wakes holiday. It was because of this overwhelming exodus of people to the seaside that neighbouring towns grew into the habit of holding their wakes weeks holiday at different times. Blackpool simply could not have accommodated the whole of Lancashire in one week.

Opposite above: London Waterloo, Saturday, 22 November 1986, Ian Allan Network SouthEast Day: Class 401 2-Bil 2090, introduced November 1937, preserved at the National Railway Museum; 4-SUB Class 405 4732 dating from 1949/50 in the background.

Opposite below: Brighton, Saturday, 10 August 1991: Class 401 2-Bil 2090.

Here is a previously Southern Railway two-car electric multiple unit which had entered service in SR lined olive green. Following nationalisation on 1 January 1948, under British Railways, Southern electric multiple units were initially out-shopped in 'early' BR green (a close resemblance to Malachite green) with later repaints from 9 July 1956 being undertaken in the later darker BR Green at Lancing Carriage Works. The inverted black triangle on yellow warning panels or full yellow ends, as seen here, was there to provide an early indication to station staff that there was no brake van at the other end of the unit. 2090 was one of a batch of units authorised for the Portsmouth No. 2 electrification scheme. It was withdrawn from service in September 1971. The classification 'Bil' indicated that the unit was provided with two lavatories; hence 'Bi-Lavatory' stock. This particular unit would have operated services from Portsmouth to Bognor Regis.

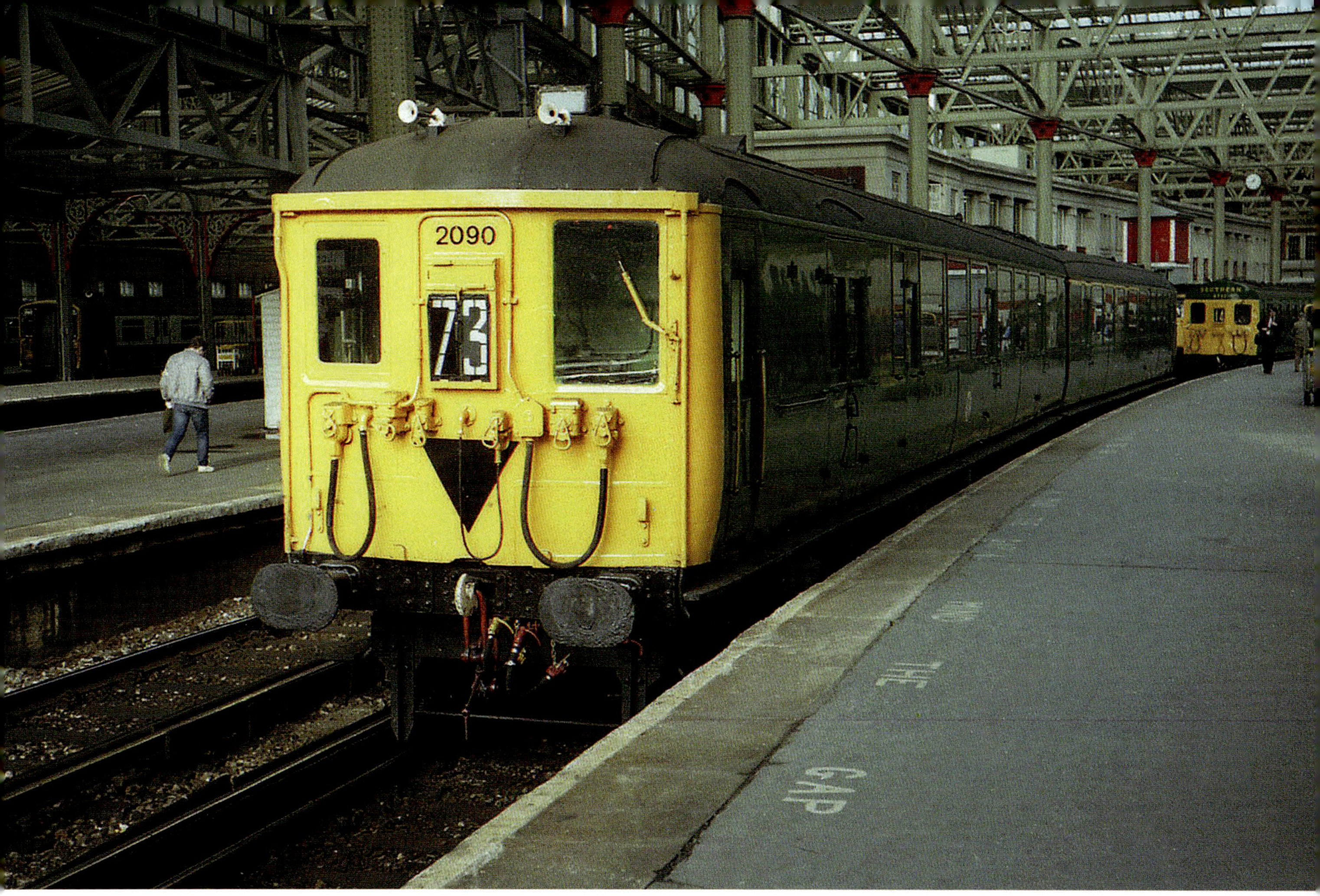
2090
73
THE
GAP

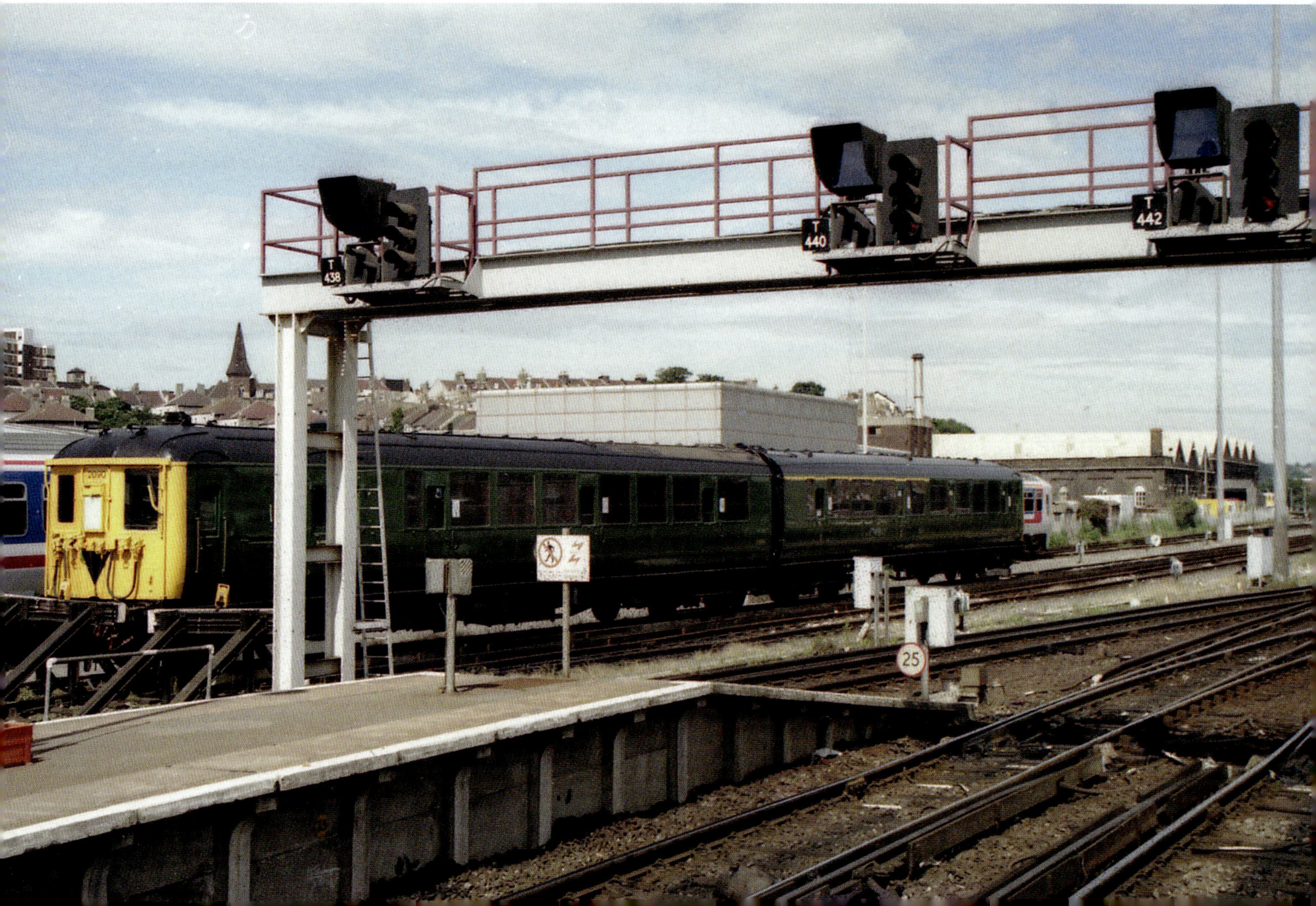
T
438
T
440
T
442
25

Bishops Bridge, South Devon Railway, Sunday, 20 May 2001: Class 25 D7612, preserved at the South Devon Railway, departs with the 18.53 Totnes to Buckfastleigh.

This two-tone green locomotive passes the fine set of semaphore signals at Bishops Bridge protecting the south end of the loop line as it rejoins the main branch in advance of Staverton station platform, which this train has just passed through. Rusting discarded permanent way fixtures such as fishplates and brackets add atmosphere to this late-spring railway landscape of the mid-evening train, and the windows will certainly be open for the enthusiasts on board to relish the sound of the Sulzer engines as they chatter away en route to their destination of Buckfastleigh, their characteristic sound reverberating off the valley through which it will pass.

Opposite above: Hood Bridge, South Devon Railway, Sunday, 24 April 2011: Class 25 D7612/25 262 hauls the 13.53 Bishops Bridge to Buckfastleigh milk and parcels train.

Another chance to consider the two-tone BR green livery applied to D7612, seen here reflected in the relatively low waters of the River Dart, unusual in spring after the customary seasonal rain showers. It stands out against the green hue of the trees and the grassy embankment and accompanied by the blood and custard of the parcels coach looks very comfortable on the slim lines of this heritage diesel.

Opposite below: Gloucester, Gloucester Rail and Transport Carnival, Sunday, 4 August 1991: foreground, Class 37/0 37197 in Civil Engineers grey and yellow ('*Dutch*') and, to the rear, from left to right, Class 35 Hymek D7018 preserved at the West Somerset Railway, Class 42 Warship D821 *Greyhound*, Class 55 Deltics D9016/55016 *Gordon Highlander* and D9000/55022 *Royal Scots Grey*.

Here the two-tone BR green is captured as worn by two locomotive classes, exhibiting the deep skirt or valance on the lower bodyside stopping just short of the cab door entrance sills, which were picked out in a lighter colour, known as Sherwood Green. Cab windscreen and side window surrounds were picked out in white. In my opinion, it may suit the Deltics best as befits their longer cab nose, and a significantly deeper application of the Sherwood Green. All three liveries on display here look attractive in their own style. It's a rare line-up offered by this feast of heritage diesels from both Eastern and Western regions of British Railways.

BR LONDON AND SOUTH EASTERN 'JAFFA-CAKE'

Dover Priory, Thursday, 30 August 1990: Class 419 DMLV (41)9010 stabled.

The product which provided the nickname for this livery is now known as McVitie's 'Jaffa Cakes *The Original'*, so named because of the distinctive layer of orange flavoured jam in these cakes (or biscuits as some would call them) which remain in our food stores. The livery was applied to several South Eastern sector CEP electric multiple units and worn by some of the MLV (Motor Luggage Van) units based at Ramsgate. They were needed as the amount of luggage accommodation available in the London to Dover boat trains was restricted, and these single coach MLVs contained two luggage compartments which provided useful additional space for those passengers with 'especially abundant' luggage. They could operate away from the electrified third rail thanks to their being fitted with on-board traction batteries, which could be recharged when the unit was drawing power from the third rail. They were withdrawn within two years of this photograph after Dover Western Docks had closed and the consequent withdrawal of boat trains to that Dover terminus. Many saw further service in departmental use.

BR MAROON

Plymouth, Saturday, 26 June 2010: Class 52 'Western' D1015 *Western Champion* in a light engine movement from Exeter to Par.

This locomotive would haul Steam Dreams 'The Cornish Riviera' 09.07 London Paddington from Par to Penzance. The train had operated under steam with 6024 *King Edward I* from London Paddington to Exeter St Davids (arriving 40 minutes late there) and with 5029 *Nunney Castle* onwards from Exeter to Par. The 'Western' had joined 6024 *King Edward I* from Taunton to Exeter as it was 'suffering from steaming problems' on the outward leg, resulting in unplanned assistance being provided from Taunton to Exeter by D1015.

This 'Western' had worn Golden Ochre livery from January 1963 until the summer of 1965 and from November 1965 until May 1968 it wore this maroon livery with standard yellow warning panels. Thereafter, until its withdrawal in December 1976, it wore BR blue with full yellow ends.

BR PROVINCIAL LIGHT BLUE

Above: Lincoln Central, Saturday, 28 February 1987: Gloucester RCW Class 100 'Stourton Saloon' ER General Manager's Saloon, at the east end of the station attached to a Class 31.

This unusual conversion of ex-Scottish Region 56300 and 51122, here renumbered in the departmental fleet as 975637 and 975664, both Gloucester RCW Class 100 DMU vehicles, formed what was known as the 'Stourton Saloon' belonging to the BR Eastern Region General Manager after they were taken into departmental stock in 1978. They were sent for scrap in 1990.

Opposite above: Nottingham Midland, Saturday, 1 March 1986: Class 150 150109, new to service October 1985, awaits departure with the 11.30 to Grantham.

The Provincial livery here looks smart as worn by this new train. The white lower half is relieved by the broad dark blue band and the pale blue upper looks a comfortable colour match. The livery was mainly applied to second generation diesel multiple units, especially the Class 142 and 143 'Pacers', Class 150 'Sprinters' and Class 158s. It seems to have been a short-lived colour scheme, somewhat overlooked by photographers as it was not applied to locomotives.

Below: Llandudno Junction, Saturday, 14 August 1993: Two Class 151 Metro-Cammell prototype 3-car dmus, 151 001 and 151 002, are seen stored withdrawn from service.

These interesting units, built 1985, carried a unique version of Provincial light blue livery. They were trialled on local services in the Derby area, including along the Matlock branch. Withdrawn in March 1989 without any further examples being built, they seem to have been considered an alternative to the Class 150s which had established their presence countrywide during their short time in service.

BR RAILFREIGHT DISTRIBUTION

Above: St Blazey Turntable, Sunday, 22 April 1990: from left to right, Class 37/5 37669, 37/0 37101 (based at Tinsley) and Class 37/5 37672 *Freight Transport Association*.

Here, Class 37 37101 in the centre carries the BR Railfreight Distribution roundel colours. Based at several depots in the north east for moving heavy freight, in the late 1970s it worked on notably rare occasions on passenger services from Newcastle to Swansea and from Sheffield to Blackpool. In the early 1980s it had the distinction of hauling some passenger services from London Liverpool Street to Cambridge and King's Lynn, and in the mid-1980s between Cardiff and Bristol. On one occasion, which must have turned a few heads, in December 1987 it was sharing duties on the Lickey Incline banking the Class 47-hauled 18.38 Paignton to Glasgow Central between Bromsgrove and Blackwell (along with Class 37 37306).

Opposite above: Exeter Riverside, Wednesday, 21 April 1993: Class 37/5 37672 *Freight Transport Association* in Railfreight Distribution decals, accompanied by a second class 37/5, await the signal to pull away with the daily Burngullow to Irvine ECC train, which is bypassed on the main line by an Intercity livery Class 47 hauling the 12.08 Plymouth to Manchester Piccadilly.

In the previous photograph we saw the cab of 37672 in BR Railfreight Grey large logo with red stripe livery. Here it is a few years later in BR Railfreight Distribution roundel livery. This was certainly one of the highlight long distance freight movements in the South West. The sheep may be blissfully grazing their grass, but their peace will soon be shattered by the sound of these powerful English Electric locomotives powering away northwards. Mind you, how lucky they are to be able to enjoy the sights and sounds of all the trains that pass by their feeding territory. Maybe their ears are attuned to awaiting the cacophony of sound to be emitted. Certainly, it is entirely worthwhile before the shearer arrives – or maybe even worse a fateful end as lunch on a plate for a contented diner in an Exeter restaurant.

Below: Teignmouth, Friday, 4 August 1989: Class 37/0 37055 passes alongside the Teign Estuary with the 12.10 Tavistock Junction to Gloucester Speedlink service with two china clay wagons and a single sliding wall Railfreight-branded VGA wagon.

    Kept clean, BR Railfreight Distribution roundel livery appeared business-like and certainly a challenge to plain BR blue. Quite whether the idea was to promote such short length trip-freights such as this remains questionable for surely it is not earning its keep here. The setting remains unspoilt although a basic wire fence partly limits the scope for photographs, though is not too intrusive. Viewers can follow activity along the railway line via a handy webcam online.

BR RAILFREIGHT RED STRIPE LARGE LOGO GREY

Menheniot, Saturday, 7 April 1990: Class 37/5 37674 passes with a west-bound civil engineers train at around midday.

A typical Cornish railway scene from the 1990s with the traditional signal box, now disused, and the Class 37 working a daytime civil engineers' train probably back to St Blazey. It was all very much taken for granted and as photographers often realise later, no longer to be repeated and now part of history. What may seem the norm today, is tomorrow's past and often it is only in hindsight that we value something for the merit it fully deserves. Such was a harsh lesson from the Beeching closures, though fortunately the Cornish main line survived any threat of closure.

BR TRAINLOAD FREIGHT COAL

Cardiff Central, Wednesday, 17 February 1993: Class 37/7 37800 *Glo Cymru* with a mid-morning coal train formed of HAA wagons, awaiting departure probably for Llanwern.

In the 1970s and 1980s, it was not unusual to see triple headed Class 37s storming through Cardiff Central on a Sunday afternoon with lengthy coal trains. Such became synonymous with the movement of Welsh coal. As the pits closed, so also the number and length of coal trains gradually reduced until the mining of coal in any quantity was considered uneconomic and eventually rendered obsolete. Now we live in a time when there are serious questions as to where our heritage steam railway lines can access quality coal for their steam locomotives, and poor quality coal is already causing problems for the firemen and drivers with consequent poorer performance of the locomotives in service. The four stylised lumps of coal in black on the yellow background of this dedicated Roundel act as a commemoration of the importance that coal as a fuel once held.

BR TRAINLOAD FREIGHT CONSTRUCTION

Above: Gloucester, Gloucester Rail and Transport Carnival, Sunday, 4 August 1991: In the foreground is Class 56 56038 *Western Mail* which leads Class 37/7 37891 hauling Pathfinder Tours' 'Sharpness Shuttle.' In the background is Class 37 37350, in BR green.

On 15 October 1987, the Trainload Business Sectors were formed. Trainload Freight constituted four sub-sectors: coal, petroleum, metals and construction. Each sub-sector of the operation was given their own two-colour Roundel design of two overlapping squares. The sharp chevrons on this design illustrated here resemble sheets of metal. The Class 37/7 locomotives could be especially seen working heavy coal trains and sheet metal and coils trains along the branch lines of the South Wales valleys, and famously serving the collieries which were to be found at the end of such lines which were notable for their heavy gradients.

Opposite above: Gloucester, Gloucester Rail and Transport Carnival, Sunday, 4 August 1991: Class 33s, left 33064 in BR Trainload Freight Construction livery, and 'right', 33102 in BR blue setting out to collect charter train stock ready for its return to London Waterloo.

Here is an interesting comparison between two class 33s, with the more recent and clean silver grey paintwork embellished with the attractive roundel proving equally colourful and maybe more eye-catching when compared to the BR blue which has lasted for so much longer. Those benefiting from travelling behind them may not enjoy such an opportunity to select a preference as that provided for lineside photographers.

Plympton, Monday, 10 May 2021: Locomotive Services Ltd. Class 37/5 37688 passes with empty coaching stock, 12.45 Crewe to Plymouth Laira depot.

This is an interesting train formation; the Class 37 is in charge of a very fine array of BR Trainload Freight Construction livery, as seen in the previous photograph, and immediately behind it is one of the Statesman Rail Rake Pullmans, MK2 BSO 9479 in Pullman Umber/Cream, acting as a barrier coach to the main set of ex-East Midland Railway's HST trailer stock which would be henceforth be formed within new 'Castle' HST sets combined with ex-Great Western Railway HST power cars.

BRITISH STEEL BLUE

Plymouth, Tuesday, 14 July 1998: Class 60 60033 *Tees Steel Express* in British Steel blue livery operating a mid-afternoon west-bound mixed freight train. It is most likely a Cliff Vale to St Blazey service. This conveyed the empty polybulks from Bescot and/or from Exeter Riverside along with any other freight that may have needed to go west.

Class 60s rarely reached beyond Exeter Riverside but here an even more unusual visitor is extending its wings west. This locomotive was named *Tees Steel Express* and repainted in special British Steel blue livery in July 1997 to mark the close links between EWS and British Steel. British Steel branding was also applied to the bodyside with a grey EWS logo and name on the cab side. 60006 also received the same treatment and the intention was for the two locomotives to work iron ore trains as a pair – though inevitably they also worked disparate duties to other locations. Introduced in the early 1990s, eventually the Class 66s replaced this Class as they were more reliable and flexible. As few as fifteen were in service by 2009 although there has been more recently an increase in their duties, shared out between several operators.

CALEDONIAN SLEEPER

Edinburgh Waverley, Thursday, 3 September 2020: Class 92 92018, stabled.

This locomotive 'in its Caledonian midnight teal livery', has the distinguished benefit of hauling the prestigious Caledonian Sleeper service, unveiled in March 2015 and formed as one of four new trains built by the train manufacturer CAF, offering four levels of comfort to intending passengers wishing to travel on the Sleeper service including 'Classic rooms,' en-suite 'Caledonian Doubles' and 'Comfort seats'. This was all a result of a decision by the Scottish government to separate the Caledonian Sleeper service from the main ScotRail franchise. The livery is a deep, dark green colour with a white stag motif (inspired by the nickname of the Fort William to London route, which was once known as *The Deerstalker*). The white stag identity has five point antlers which represent the services' three Highland and two Lowland destinations. It is quite a change from the intended use of the powerful Class 92s on Channel Tunnel services, and it gives them a chance to redeem their sometimes tarnished reliability record.

Fort William, Thursday, 16 September 2021: Class 73/9 73971 with GBRF Class 66/7 66741 with empty Caledonian Sleepers stock.

These specially-rebuilt ex-Southern Region Class 73 electro-diesels have been fitted with 1,600hp MTU diesel engine power units similar (if lower powered) to those used in Class 43 HSTs. All these locos received the same green/white stag livery as the coaches, also with large body-side antler graphics. They are now fitted with multiple working control and can work with class 66 and 67 locos and can also work with un-rebuilt Class 73s. Pairs of these were intended to haul the Caledonian Sleeper trains from Edinburgh and Glasgow to their Highland destinations, replacing the Class 67s previously used. In practice, they proved inadequate for this and now provide electric train heating, while the powerful Class 66 provides the requisite tractive effort to manage the train's journey up the demanding gradients. One of the main problems were the new alternators which suffered from vibration problems, particularly when at full power. The coaches' design and specification have revolutionised the concept of quality and comfort in Caledonian Sleeper services. However, there have been unflattering reviews by some commentators raising several concerns about inadequacies of the new sleeper compartments when compared to the previous Mk 3 stock, echoed by some passengers with whom I conversed.

It is interesting to note that a similar resurgence of overnight Sleeper services has taken place in nearby Western Europe, after Austrian Railways (ÖBB) reintroduced long distance services from Austria to Germany, France and Holland previously withdrawn by German Railways (DB). One such service is that introduced in December 2021 linking Paris with Vienna via Karlsruhe and Stuttgart, operated by ÖBB as part of its expanding Nightjet network, During the same month, a duo of services was introduced by SNCF (French Railways) providing a revitalised Paris-Austerlitz night train bound for Briançon and another train for Tarbes and Lourdes, conveying coaches for Latour de Carol and Cerbère/Port-Bou. There clearly remains an increasing demand for overnight sleepers, despite the alternatives of high speed daytime travel.

CENTRAL TRAINS

Lincoln Central, Thursday, 27 April 2000: Class 158/7 158797 in Central Trains livery prepares to depart with the 16.18 service to Manchester Airport.

An appropriately bright green diesel multiple unit is here seen in the centre of Lincoln green territory. It is eye-catching and carries the phone number of the operator very prominently. Central Trains was initially allocated seventeen units in the 158/7 series, these having previously constituted the Regional Railways Central allocation. Central Trains served a vast network understandably centred on the West Midlands conurbation but extending out to East Anglia, Lincolnshire, The Potteries, and along the Sheffield, Manchester and Liverpool (Cheshire Lines) axis.

CHILTERN TRAINS

Above: London Marylebone, Saturday, 27 May 2000 : Chiltern Railways Class 168 'Clubman' 168005 in Chiltern Railways livery awaits service later in the morning.

This diesel unit was one of the first batch of Clubman 168/0 trains ordered by Chiltern Railways and these were the first units ordered by any train operating company since the privatisation of the UK industry in 1996. They were delivered as three-car sets but later lengthened to four-car sets. The Chiltern white and blue may be described as conservative when compared to the Network SouthEast colours applied to other trains serving Marylebone during and prior to this era, and from which it was adapted. They would have been seen regularly providing commuter services to Aylesbury.

Opposite above: Warwick, Saturday, 7 August 2021: Chiltern Mainline livery Class 68 68013 departs in push-mode with Chiltern Railways' 13.37 Birmingham Moor Street to London Marylebone.

The Chiltern Mainline Silver services, which are a selected number of services between Kidderminster/Birmingham and London Marylebone, feature class 68 locomotives, with hauled coaching sets formed of Mk3 Driving Van Trailers and Mk3 plug door fitted carriages. There are six class 68 locomotives allocated to these services. Of the six carriages, five are standard and one is business class. The trains are well used and there appears to be plenty of regional travel as well as commuter traffic. Based on a recent journey on this particular train in the photograph, it is a smart and business-like presentation of rolling stock, livery and interior high standard of comfort and cleanliness.

CIVIL ENGINEERS

Below: Royal Albert Bridge, Saturday, 23 November 1991: Class 50s, nearest to camera 50008 *Thunderer* in blue standard livery and 'second', 50015 *Valiant* in Civil Engineering livery, at the rear of Pathfinder Tours' 'The Valiant Thunderer' en route from Manchester Piccadilly to Newquay.

50015 *Valiant* was the only class 50 to be painted into BR Civil Engineers 'Dutch' livery. As such it attracted much interest for its unique livery in the Class 50 fleet. Both of these locomotives have passed into preservation, and this reinforces the popularity of the class during its working life. Their appeal among the rail enthusiast community was equally earned in the north west, when pairs worked the Crewe to Glasgow section of services from London pre-electrification of that part of the West Coast main line, and in the West Country on express passenger services – earning their well-deserved recognition after replacing the very popular 'Western' Class on these.

Staverton, South Devon Railway, Thursday, 3 June 2021: Civil Engineers grey Class 33 33002 pauses with the 18.10 Totnes to Buckfastleigh.

Class 33 33002 gleams in the early evening summer sunshine in its freshly applied grey livery as it approaches Staverton on the final service of the day, from Totnes Riverside to Buckfastleigh, with six carriages in tow reflecting the busy services during the Whit half-term week. Train lengths were increased to accommodate the need for social distancing during the pandemic. This locomotive had carried such a livery in the late 1980s and early 1990s.

Opposite below: Laira Depot, Thursday, 13 June 1991: Class 47/4 47976 *Aviemore Centre* (ex-47546) with DB975280 Mobile Track Assessment Unit (support and accommodation vehicle), formerly Test Coach *Mercury*, and DB975081 Structure Gauging Train Driving and Instrumentation vehicle, formerly Test Coach *Hermes*.

This distinctive Structure Gauging Train helps measure what is known as route loading gauge to ensure that trains using a specific route can pass clear of all structures, principally over-bridges and tunnels but also features such as station platforms, canopies and overhead or lineside equipment. The train also measures the distance between pairs of tracks ensuring that passing trains will not foul the loading gauge. Therefore it essentially checks both the height and width profile of the railway. In the centre of the train is a specially-built four wheel structure-gauging optical vehicle. It deploys specialist laser and light technology using a dual-triangulation system with lights and cameras to give a clear measure of the railway infrastructure. DB975081 was specially converted to a driving trailer vehicle for use in this train.

This train was in use until the early 2000s when Network Rail introduced a new formation using converted Mk2 carriages.

COLAS RAIL

Below: Silverton, Sunday, 31 October 2021: Colas Rail Class 70/8 70812 passes with the two-hour early 14.47 Exeter St Davids to Westbury civil engineer's train.

The flooded field reflects the intense rains of the previous week – my car traversed (and survived) flood waters of 18 inches driving down Devon lanes leading to this rural picturesque location near Tiverton. The times of the trains returning from substantial track replacement work at Exmouth Junction were as unpredictable as the weather. However, rather than wait for the hourly scheduled returning engineering trains, they were sensibly flighted, with three Up trains passing in procession, and the sunshine obligingly counteracted the sod's law that usually applies – namely that the sun goes behind a cloud as soon as the train required for the camera's shutter to click turns up.

Opposite above and opposite below: Newton St Cyres, Thursday, 29 April 2021: Colas Class 66/8 66848 leads and Colas Class 66/8 66847 pushes the heavy stone ballast train forming the 07.03 Westbury to Crediton for the Okehampton branch, with both engines working hard.

The quiet of this part of the mid-Devon countryside was regularly disturbed during the spring of 2021 when a procession of civil engineering trains made their way towards the section of the Okehampton line north of Yeoford which was being entirely relaid, ready for the start of regular passenger services in the autumn. This train had combined ballast wagons in both Network Rail and civil engineering yellow liveries. Had it been a little later in the day, those observing the trains from the nearby brew pub would have been able to see the same train returning to Exeter Riverside yard after delivering its materials, although they may not have been aware of the reasons for such, but it no doubt proved a discussion point over a pint of their favourite.

Devonport Cutting, Friday, 9 April 2021: Colas Rail Class 67 67023 leads the Network Rail New Measurement Train with 67027 at the rear, forming the 06.08 Reading Triangle to Paignton via Penzance (here on its return from Penzance).

This variation of Colas Class 67s being used in place of the usual HST power cars that operate this yellow train on its monthly visit down the Cornish main line certainly catches the eye. The angular shape of the Class 67s does not always facilitate different livery styles but it seems to work here. The surrounding gardens and allotments clearly give the impression that spring has arrived and pay their own colourful tribute in kind.

Opposite: Weston Mill Viaduct, Friday, 11 March 2022: Colas Class 70 70801 leads the 12.00 Penwithers Junction to Westbury civil engineers train with Class 70 70811 at the rear.

Passengers crossing this high viaduct can see a fine view of the Royal Navy vessels at berth or manoeuvering into the River Tamar at the Devonport Dockyard complex. The viaduct appears to have received a smart coat of blue paint which stands out well on this fine afternoon. The early spring sunshine highlights the intertwining framework of the viaduct through the shadows cast on the rails which it conveys at this location.

There is a view taken in July 2000 of a Midland Mainline livery HST passing the same location on page 149.

CROSSCOUNTRY

Below: Laira Embankment, Tuesday, 21 January 2020: CrossCountry HST power cars with 43285 leading, with an intermediate coach, forming a trip from Laira T&RSM depot to Plymouth station for the purpose of turning the coach via Laira triangle on return.

Winter light can be special for photographers as, caught in the low level sun, side-on images can reveal details that are lost in very strong and overhead light emitted by summer sunshine. The remnants of the overnight frost on the sleepers close to the salty estuary suggest a previous cold clear night. The tide is out and the water in the mudflats low enough to reveal the wreck of a boat's hull. Such features each add interest to this image of a relatively unusual train formation.

Bodmin Parkway, Saturday, 26 June 2010: CrossCountry HST power car 43321, evidently in freshly applied livery, at the rear of the departing 09.27 Newquay to Dundee.

This is certainly a long distance train, and the travellers on board have the good fortune of High Speed Train coaches with comfortable seats, a carpeted floor and wide windows accompanied by a smooth and steady ride – the alternative of the full distance journey on board a 'Voyager' would be closer to an experience of purgatory. The CrossCountry HSTs have if anything gained admiration and 'street cred' during their maturity, especially after the withdrawal of the First Great Western sets, and their extended journeys into Cornwall add further appeal. The train will have already provided an absorbing journey through some spectacular curves and landscapes for those travelling with it along the Newquay branch. Summer Saturdays in past years often meant a more reduced service along the branch than on a weekday, in order to accommodate the through trains from and to London and the North East.

Powderham, Saturday, 26 September 2020: CrossCountry HST with power car 43378 at the rear passes with the 15.26 Plymouth to York.

The Exe estuary forms a picturesque backdrop for passengers on this train to enjoy before they arrive at Exeter (seen in the distance) and they will very shortly pass the Turf Lock pub at the junction of Exeter Canal and the estuary, the lock of which can be seen just beyond the front power car. The only way of reaching this popular hotel and bar is by foot, cycle or boat, and they may well prefer to be there supping a pint of local ale and enjoying the late summer sunshine than perhaps returning from an enjoyable fortnight in Torbay, South Devon or Cornwall. The Devon main line is very busy at this location, with a mix of local and regional trains as well as long distance services.

DB CARGO UK

Foley Park, Severn Valley Railway, Thursday, 18 May 2017: DB Class 60 60100 at the rear of the 14.20 Bewdley to Kidderminster ascends the gradient towards Bewdley tunnel.

It was inevitable that with the purchase of EWS in 2007, the UK railway scene would see the distinctive red already applied to Deutsche Bahn's locomotive fleet in Germany bestowing those of Britain's locomotives that now came under DB Schenker's ownership. So it was that Class 59 59206 was the first to be adorned in DB Schenker livery, in January 2009. In March 2016, DB Schenker was rebranded as DB Cargo UK, and the livery accompanied that rebranding. Interestingly, it was from the early years of the second decade of the millennium that freight trains in Germany became increasingly hauled by private operators, so that the ubiquitous red became less evident in that country. Similarly in Britain at the same time, new private railfreight haulage companies surfaced to challenge the standardised colours of EWS.

Laira Embankment, Monday, 25 January 2021: DB Class 66s 66020 and 66107 top and tail the 11.58 Westbury to St Erth civil engineers train.

Making a colourful display on this cool winter's day, with a smattering of snow on the nearby moor, the high tide fills the Plym estuary and the low level of the sun highlights the bright red livery worn by these class 66s. In fact, the driver can enjoy a relatively scenic journey after passing through Plymouth as the train's route will cross the River Tamar over the Royal Albert Bridge followed by several viaducts crossing creeks and estuarial inlets before reaching Liskeard and then descending through the attractive Glynn Valley Forest between Liskeard and Bodmin in Cornwall. Those woodlands feature prominently within the landscape on both sides of the river Fowey, and are glimpsed in the photograph of Bodmin Parkway, Saturday, 26 June 2010, featuring the CrossCountry HST.

Royal Albert Bridge, Thursday, 10 February 2022: DB Cargo Class 66/0 66148 *Maritime Intermodal 7* leaves the bridge with the 11:51 Parkandillack to Exeter Riverside China Clay, eventually destined for Bescot.

More often to be found serving rail services from DP World London Gateway, the small dedicated fleet of blue Maritime livery Class 66 locomotives deliver daily container trains to Trafford Park near Manchester and to Wakefield in addition to existing services to Felixstowe and Southampton. The dedicated 'Maritime' branding commenced in April 2019 with the launch of Maritime Intermodal, profiling an agreement between Maritime Transport Ltd (Maritime) and DB Cargo (UK) Ltd to increase rail freight capacity, with the first two named Class 66s *Maritime Intermodal One* and *Maritime Intermodal Two*. This visit to the South West by one of these standard locomotives wearing the distinctive livery is certainly an infrequent event and the winter's afternoon light helps to highlight the weekly east-bound freight.

DEPARTMENTAL: DM&EE MECHANICAL AND ELECTRICAL ENGINEERING DEPARTMENT

Bury Bolton Street, East Lancashire Railway, Saturday, 2 June 1990: RDB 975003 *Laboratory 16* and 975004 *Gemini* Derby/Cowlairs works two-car battery electric unit. This was owned by the Mechanical and Electrical Engineering Department's (DM&EE) Testing Section and the Research & Development Division (R&DD) based at the Railway Technical Centre (RTC) at Derby.

  This battery railcar was formed of two vehicles semi-permanently coupled together and given the description of Motor Coach RDB975003 and Driving Trailer RDB 975004, having previously been originally BR Sc79998 and Sc79999. It saw use on the Ballater branch where it commenced service in 1958 and was acquired by the R&DD in 1966. It carried the dedicated DM&EE livery applied to their fleet of railway vehicles. Appropriately it now resides at the Royal Deeside Railway where it carries a superbly restored full BR green livery.

DEPARTMENTAL SANDITE AND DE-ICING

Gatwick Airport, Monday, 25 October 1999: Class 930 Sandite and De-icing Unit 930 011 (975602 and 975603) ex-Southern Region 4-SUB motor coaches Driving Motor Brake Deicing Vans, south-bound mid-morning on RHTT (Rail Head Treatment Train) duties.

This converted ex-BR Southern Region commuter stock electric multiple unit carries early Railtrack bronze, white and grey livery. It gave a contrast to the familiar Network SouthEast and Connex livery applied to trains passing this location during this era and provided an opportunity to see an old veteran unit still earning its keep, even if no longer involved in carrying passengers on board.

DOCKLANDS LIGHT RAILWAY

Millwall Inner Dock and South Quay, Friday, 29 July 1994: Docklands Light Rail bi-directional single-articulated Electric Multiple Unit crosses between South Quay and Crossharbour stations.

This location was once the site of the Central Granary, built 1901-3. Canary Wharf dominates this scene, with its 800ft height and fifty floors. I recall my first trip on this ground breaking railway, when Canary Wharf was the only main feature on an otherwise huge building site in various stages of completion, with some of the dock basins completely isolated and underdeveloped. The trains had their own novelty for, being automated – hence without a driver's cab – it was possible to obtain a driver's view of the line ahead or to the rear. There is a small driver's console concealed behind a locked panel at each outer car end from which the Passenger Service Agent can drive the train when necessary. The nature of the line with its sharp curves and short climbs added to the intrigue along with stations at which the train automatically stopped, but with nothing yet built to be served. It was interesting to travel as far as Island Gardens to see the full extent of the docklands railway and the rather small houses being built for no doubt a very handsome fee. Station names such as 'Mudchute' also added to the curiosity offered by this pioneering railway network.

Above and opposite: Heron Quays and South Quay, Monday, 12 March 2018: Docklands Light Rail bi-directional single-articulated Electric Multiple Units.

Capturing the very essence of the Docklands Light Railway in the second decade of the twenty-first century, exhibiting its impressions of ultra-modernistic office buildings and attractive docklands waterways, a combination of leisure and commerce is exuded in this essentially new city. The DLR now provides services to Beckton, Stratford and Woolwich to the East and North East and Docklands, Lewisham and Greenwich to the South. New Bombardier trains, needed for network extensions and three-car service on the Bank to Lewisham route, were delivered between December 2007 and September 2008. They feature a much redesigned exterior and interior, with larger windows and doors and in the interior, more leg room. These newer units also provide improved acceleration, and are designed to better accommodate faster boarding and alighting. Those who use the network will be aware of the daily overcrowding despite the very frequent service that reflects the great success of this light rail system amidst the constantly growing and developing nature of the environment with which it entwines – one that has risen literally from a previous wasteland. Note that the red and blue of the train seen in the 1990s photograph has now been modified to overall red with a curving blue banner.

DIRECT RAIL SERVICES

Above: Bodmin Parkway, Saturday, 26 June 2010: a pair of DRS Class 37s, front: 37259, second: 37218 sweep through with Spitfire Rail Tours' 06.45 Gloucester to Penzance 'The Kernow Explorer'

The noise of this pair of locomotives impressively shatters the quiet of the wooded Glynn valley, although they are certainly offering a welcome sound to the enthusiasts on board, and equally to lineside photographers and maybe even the east-bound passengers on the opposite platform. DRS has certainly earned a reliable reputation for using these fine English Electric locomotives on passenger trains, fulfilling diagrams where there has been a shortage of units, such as in Cumbria and East Anglia. They are ever popular, with everyday passengers benefiting from the comfort of proper hauled carriages as opposed to the bouncy ride of the Pacer or Sprinter whose place they have taken. Almost forty of the class are preserved.

Opposite above: Ipswich Stabling Point, Friday, 30 May 2008: a mid-morning view of DRS Class 37/6 37606 in Direct Rail Services livery, stabled with the Network Rail New Measurement Train. To the right can be seen Freightliner Class 66/5 66587 and Freightliner Class 66/5 66576 *Hamburg Sud Advantage*.

There is usually something of interest either at the stabling point or passing through Ipswich station, both passenger and freight (especially from Felixstowe). It is intriguing that yellow livery has been adopted for rail engineers' motive power in many European countries – it is a sensible and safe colour enabling enhanced visual presence of such traction when out on duties where track is attended to.

Below: Stirling, 10 September 2021: Class 68 68006 with the 13.10 Inverness to Mossend Tesco Express.

The 'Tesco Extra' pool of Chinese-built distinctive curtain-sided wagons wearing Tesco/Stobart Rail 'Less CO2' branding has been financed with the assistance of a substantial Freight Facilities Grant acquired in 2008 from the Scottish Executive. Since then, this train has served the Highlands via an intermodal terminal at Inverness. At that time, it was hauled by Class 66/4 locomotives and is now in the hands of Class 68 diesels. It adds a colourful freight train to the usual diet of passenger trains along the Highland main line and frequently features in railway media photographs reflecting the majesty of the Highland scenery. It looks equally impressive in the fine architecture of Stirling station. While there had been a station at Stirling since 1848, as more lines opened, operated by different companies, the station proved inadequate. In 1889, the Caledonian Railway and North British Railway agreed to enlarge the station and sought powers for additional land. The current station finally opened in 1915.

Whalley Viaduct, Wednesday, 6 October 2021: Class 68 68016 heads south with the 12.46 Carlisle to Crewe Basford Hall civil engineers train.

I have a love/hate relationship with the weather at this location. Whilst not difficult to reach with a short diversion from the M6 motorway, the weather tends to be sunny on arrival but by the time the train preferred for photography turns up, usually delayed, the sun has gone behind a cloud, only to emerge once the train has passed. Fortunately, it remained bright for this train and actually sunny for the preceding north-bound Colas Class 70 hauled 09.18 Mount Sorrell to Carlisle.

The long viaduct with its 48 round arches offers several photographic options with the afternoon lighting favouring this view. Built to carry the Bolton, Blackburn, Clitheroe and West Yorkshire Railway, it opened in 1850. It is built with red and blue brick and crosses the River Calder, 21.3m above the river for a distance of 620m, exerting an impressive impact on the surrounding landscape.

EAST COAST TRAINS

Stonehaven, Friday, 15 April 2011: National Express East Coast Railways HST with power car 43319 leading passes with the 14.50 Aberdeen to London King's Cross.

This train here passes the signal box at Stonehaven which is a Caledonian Railway (Northern Division) Type 2 box installed in 1901 and sited prominently on the platform to the left of the main station building. Noteworthy is the timber staircase from the platform up to the signal box cabin. The LNER livery worn by this HST later in the decade was certainly more eye-catching. The first HST power cars to be reliveried for the start of the National Express East Coast Railways franchise in December 2007 were 43300 and 43238 and in clean fresh silver and white paint certainly appeared smart and appealing. The large amount of white on the carriages and on a third of the power car did however start to look grubby after several years of intense use. By early 2009, it became clear that National Express would default on their franchise with the InterCity East Coast train operating company, and operations passed to the publicly-owned East Coast Main Line Company on 14 November 2009, ending in February 2015. The 'National Express' branding was replaced by 'East Coast' branding but the colour scheme remained the same on some power cars (as seen here) for some time after a distinctive East Coast livery was introduced. This livery was replaced by that of InterCity East Coast when that new franchise began in March 2015. This was when Virgin Trains East Coast took over operating the main line routes from King's Cross.

EAST MIDLANDS RAILWAY

Arley, Severn Valley Railway, Saturday, 9 October 2021: East Midlands Railway HST power cars 43277 (nearest), 43257 and 43251 stored under ownership of Colas from 22 July 2021.

Not your usual view of Arley station yard. This intrusion of High Speed Train power cars more familiar with the passengers along the East Coast and Midland main lines does not quite fit the scene, given its context of a rural traditional preservation heritage station and signal box operating semaphore signals for steam trains.

In fact, it was not long before this that these power cars had been operating along the East Coast main line for Virgin Trains East Coast while based at Edinburgh Craigentinny depot. Transferred to East Midlands Railway (EMR) for a short time after being displaced by the IET fleet which took over LNER services out of King's Cross, they undertook duties on the Midland main line – part of a project to return nine of the ex-LNER HST sets to traffic with EMR. However, Saturday, 15 May 2021 saw the end of an era for the Midland main line, with East Midlands Railway running their final HST passenger services, these trains having dominated the Midland main line over the years from London St Pancras to destinations including Leicester, Nottingham, Derby, Sheffield and Leeds. The power cars featured here were then acquired by Colas Rail from 22 July 2021 for use in supplying traction for the NMT operating from and to Derby RTC and were reported in use (by a National Rail internal source) as such in early October 2021. By November of the same year, 43257 had acquired Colas Rail yellow diamond-shaped logos on its body side. They had full fuel tanks while at Arley, and indeed saw further mainline use in their new guise. As for services along the Midland main line, from 16 May 2021, as a result of all London St Pancras to Corby services being now operated by Class 360 EMUs, there are adequate Class 222 and Class 180s to take over the former HST services to Nottingham and Leeds. Whether passengers will welcome such replacement of the popular HSTs remains to be seen.

EWS ENGLISH, WELSH & SCOTTISH RAILWAY

Forder Viaduct, Friday, 23 July 1999: EWS Class 66 66124 in EWS livery with a light engine movement west-bound, early evening. It was delivered new in June 1999. The Lynher River estuary is in the background.

The ubiquitous EWS Class 66 revolutionised freight haulage in the UK but did not please the locomotive enthusiasts, who saw many of their favourite classes of diesel decimated. It was in December 1996 that EWS was announced as the preferred bidder for the loss-making Railfreight Distribution whose businesses included international containerised freight, movement of cars and automotive components by rail. The sale, which included 157 locomotives, was concluded in March 1997. At this point, EWS controlled 90 per cent of the rail freight market. Railfreight Distribution was renamed English Welsh & Scottish Railway International on 1 December 1998. Since then, their integral colours adorning Class 66 locomotives have become a very familiar sight all over the British railway network. Where still carried, they now often look generally tired, especially with some examples working on civil engineering trains, and certainly not as bright and fresh as this Class 66. However, as workhorses, their reliability and power remain impressive and have proved a very wise investment, for which the Class 59s operated by Foster Yeoman set the trend. They have established a reputation within the railfreight industry for their versatility moving a wide variety of traffic including containers on key north/south arteries, and trainload freight including oil, aggregates, cement, steel, coal, and infrastructure trains.

Above: St Germans viaduct, Sunday, 6 December 2020: EWS liveried Class 66 66014 hauls the 09.25 Westbury to Penzance Long Rock civil engineers' ballast train.

Any train seen in this landscape will surely look interesting. It is a relatively low tide here where the River Tiddy, a small river in south-east Cornwall, widens as it forms the main tributary of the River Lynher or St Germans River as it is alternatively referred to downstream of St Germans. The train calmly passes by without intruding on the calm of the gently sunlit winter's day scene. As if to reinforce the point made accompanying the previous photograph, the Class 66s can be seen engaged in a wide variety of traffic, and the livery has remained unchanged for many of those owned by DB Cargo (the current owners of the Class 66/0 series), except for when they decide such is requisite.

Opposite above: Ipswich, Friday, 30 May 2008: EWS Class 90 90028 – on loan – hauls National Express East Anglia 10.30 Norwich to London Liverpool Street service; the coaches are in National Express East Anglia livery.

Evident here is the EWS logo consisting of three heads: the lion of England, the dragon of Wales and the stag of Scotland. It reminded viewers that the company operated in all parts of Britain. Quite whether the designers expected to see it emblazoned on a locomotive dedicated to EWS, a freight haulage company, working an express passenger service is open to question. Most of the passengers aboard this train would probably not be aware of such a detail, although photographers would certainly welcome the unusual use of such on the East Anglian main line.

Opposite below: Highley, Severn Valley Railway, Saturday, 9 October 2021: Class 31/4 31466 is stabled alongside Highley signal box. It had been repainted after completion of a three-year overhaul by the Dean Forest Diesel Association.

Proudly wearing its fresh, immaculate, paintwork perfectly demonstrating the attractive maroon and gold that composes the EWS livery, this was one of only two of the class 31 locomotives to receive such a livery, although 31255, based at the Mid-Norfolk Railway, received its coat of paint in this colour scheme after its withdrawal and when in preservation. The Class appeared in a wide variety of other colours, and most, apart from plain grey with black cab doors – a most uninspiring livery – suited these locomotives very well. An example of such may be seen in the photograph on page 44 showing Class 31/1 31190 in BR green (with white stripe) and Class 31/6 31601 in DCR (Devon and Cornwall Railway) dark green livery.

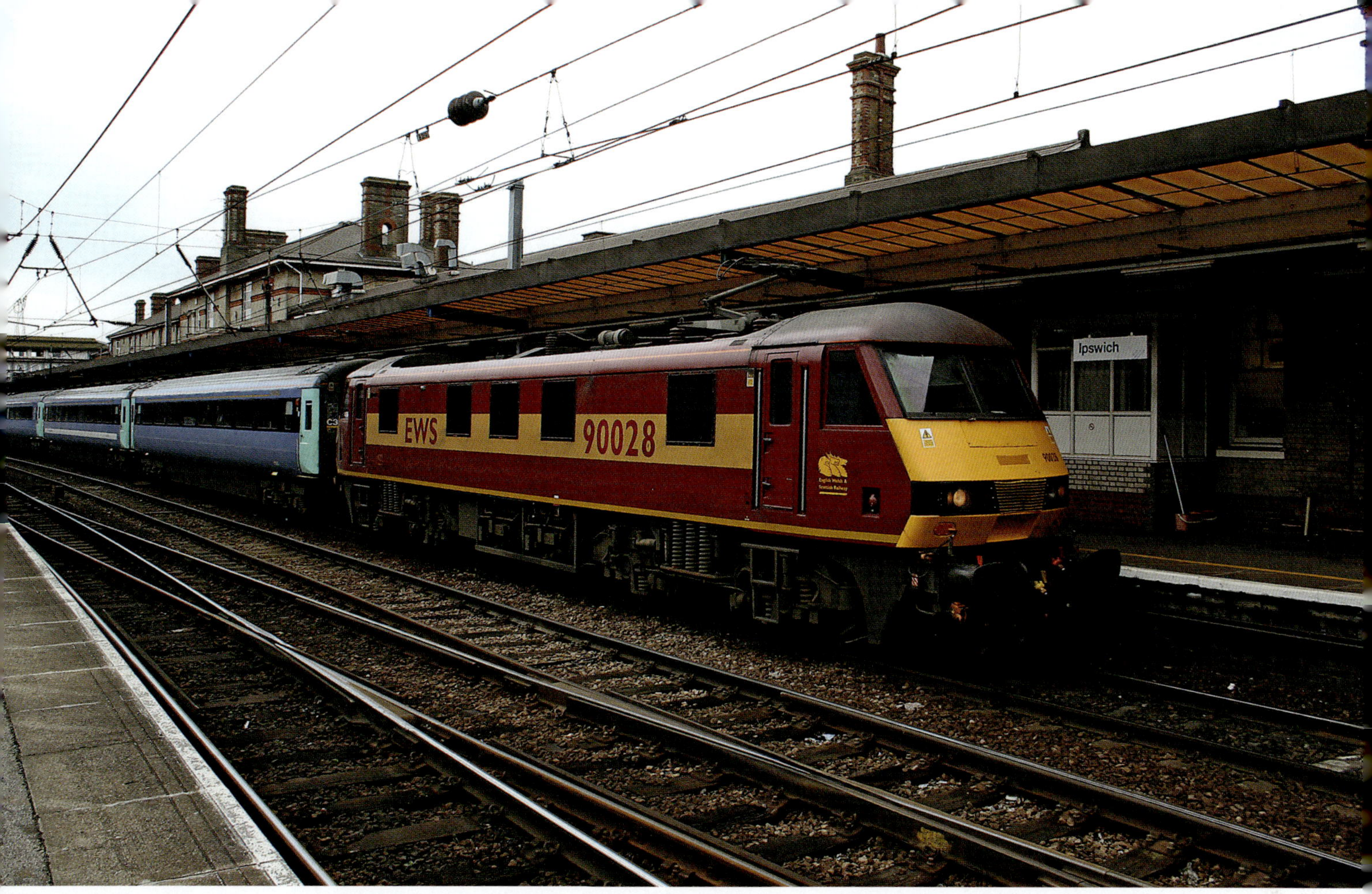
Ipswich
EWS
90028

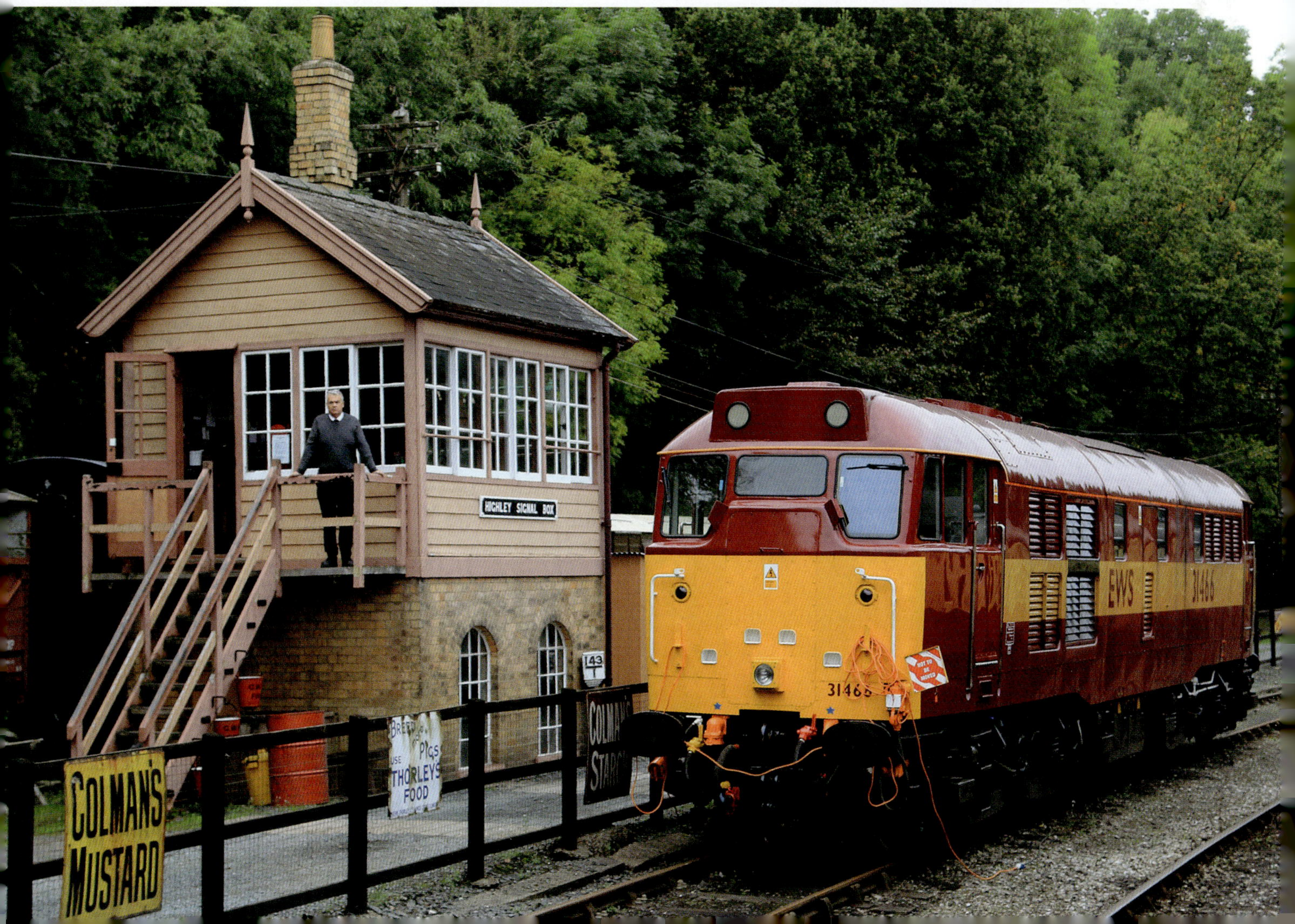
HIGHLEY SIGNAL BOX
EWS
31466
COLMAN'S
MUSTARD
USE
THORLEYS
FOOD

FIRST GREAT WESTERN

London Paddington, Thursday, 29 August 2002: Two First Great Western Class 180 'Adelante' five-car Express diesel multiple units depart with the 14.45 service to Bristol Temple Meads, late running after technical difficulties with the train doors.

This small fleet of trains had hydraulic transmission and convey therefore some continuation of the BR Western Region theme of hydraulic traction as exemplified by the Class 52 'Westerns,' Class 35 'Hymeks' and Class 42 'Warships'. They provide a comfortable ride and certainly outshine the competition's 'Voyagers'. Their Achilles' heel has been with recurring technical problems, although they have seen reliable service with several operators including First Great Western, Northern Rail (for services between Manchester and Blackpool) and Grand Central. They did reach Plymouth briefly during the summer of 2004. The blue, white and pink colours of First Group are relieved by the thick gold band, bearing the Great Western branding at the centre point, applied to HST carriage sets.

Dawlish, Saturday, 9 July 2011: First Great Western HST passes with the 10.06 London Paddington to Penzance 'The Cornish Riviera'.

The coaching set formed within this HST carries the 'Dynamic Lines' livery, a series of white, blue and pink wavy lines carried along the full length of each carriage whereas the power cars carry a plain blue livery, all of which forms a complimentary match. This was very much the standard scene at this location, where the aquamarine of the high tide's waters would remind passengers and coastal walkers alike of the close proximity of sea and train – which in later years became a significant problem thanks to climate change and increasingly stormy winters resulting in the sea wall and a section of line being effectively washed away in the storms of February 2014.

Morchard Road, Saturday, 23 July 2011: First Great Western Class 142 'Pacer' 142029, in First Great Western blue without logo/branding, arrives with the 18.27 Exmouth to Barnstaple.

This 'Pacer' looks very smart having clearly received a fresh coat of paint to replace its previous North West Trains livery borne while operating from Newton Heath depot, Manchester. In some ways this scene captures the very essence of the mid-Devon rolling countryside with a named station that suggests the nearest community to be served along 'the road' and far away from this location. Understandably the Barnstaple branch line keeps to the valleys and therefore skirts several villages which historically, for defence purposes, occupy high ground and therefore require additional transport in order to reach the nearest station – which is hardly conducive to using the service when decent highways facilitate alternative use of your car. Furthermore, to experience travel in these 'nodding donkeys' – even more basic than the usual Class 143s – would not invite a return trip. It is at least of some consolation that the nearby branch to Okehampton has received much investment and a restored service, highly popular and providing hourly trains with pairs of Class 150 'Sprinters' on Saturdays leading up to Christmas 2021 after its reopening on 20 November, the first line to be reinstated under the Department for Transport's 'Restoring your Railway' initiative.

FOSTER YEOMAN AND HANSON

Merehead Depot approach lines, Saturday, 10 July 1999: Class 59/1s left: 59103 *Village of Mells* in Hanson Group livery, centre: 59102 *Village of Chantry* in ARC livery, right: Class 59/0 59002 *Alan J Day* in Foster Yeoman livery.

A visit organised by me in my role as Fixtures Secretary for the Plymouth Railway Circle to the Mendip Rail centre of operations at Merehead maintenance depot proved a very memorable event, all thanks to the generosity of the hosts who facilitated a trip around the quarry – by our coach – and a look at the locomotives, with opportunity for some cab rides within the locality of the depot's rails.

Mendip Rail was formed in 1993 as a joint venture between the rail traffic of Foster Yeoman (which is incorporated in Aggregates Industries) and ARC (now part of the Hanson Group). This included their locomotives (including some class 08s and an American Switcher) and company branded wagons. Their class 59s became synonymous with the rail operations of Mendip Rail's limestone traffic (some 6 million tonnes every year). They were managed as a common pool and were operated with very heavy loads (up to 5,000 tonnes) to Acton and in smaller loads especially to several terminals along the South Coast and in Oxfordshire amongst other locations. Significant contracts to move stone have included more than two million tonnes for the second Prince of Wales Bridge River Severn Crossing and stone for the sea defences at Minehead. Note also front cab detail differences.

Saturday, 10 July 1999, Merehead Depot: Class 59/1 59103 *Village of Mells* in Hanson Group livery. To the rear is 59101 *Village of Whatley* in ARC livery.

One of the complex technical aspects which has assisted the haulage of such heavy loads associated with these locomotives is their 'Creep' adhesion control system. This improves adhesion through the powered wheels which are allowed to rotate or creep under controlled slip conditions. It permits carefully controlled wheel slip so that the train locomotive can manage to haul its heavy load at a sustained steady speed without the damaging wheel slip that can easily happen with such loads on slippery rails. This technical advantage proved attractive also to another of General Motors' customers, the electricity generator National Power, who purchased a small fleet of six Class 59 locomotives. The 'Creep' facility was further incorporated in the Brush built Class 60 design – locomotives designed for use with heavy trains such as fuel tanker loads.

FREIGHTLINER

Ipswich, Friday, 30 May 2008: Freightliner Class 90 90042, in Freightliner grey livery, leads Freightliner Class 86/6 86604 in Freightliner green livery (not in power) hauling a mid-morning north-bound container train to Felixstowe.

It is actually two-tone grey worn here by the Class 90, but its appearance is rather drab, even with the red triangle Freightliner logo, given a cloudy grey day – the Freightliner green and full yellow cabs carried by the veteran electric Class 86 looks so much better, as does the large yellow logo. At this time, pairs of these could be seen in regular work double-heading lengthy Freightliner services from the North West (Ditton, Trafford Park and Crewe) via the West Coast main line to the ports of East Anglia and the Thames Estuary. Infrequently they would even handle such loads single-handed. The two locomotives are from two very different eras, and while the Class 90 is bristling with newer technology, this Class 86 continued to earn its keep for nearly forty-five years after it was built, members of the Class having been built by British Railways at Doncaster (sixty locomotives) or by English Electric at Vulcan Foundry, Newton-le-Willows (forty locomotives). Mind you, the Swiss have a tendency to use a small number of much older electric locomotives in non-passenger service, partly to keep the parts from seizing up and to keep the motors maintained.

Above: Ipswich Stabling Point, Friday, 30 May 2008: From left to right, Freightliner Class 66/5 66539, Freightliner Class 66/5 66576 *Hamburg Sud Advantage*, Freightliner Class 86/6 86604, Freightliner Class 66/5 66580, all in Freightliner green livery. Early afternoon.

It is worth commenting that Freightliner had a fleet of sixteen Class 86/6s including ten of the ex-Railfreight Distribution Class 86/6s for freight haulage. They were previously Class 86/4s with their train heating capabilities removed, with other modifications, and with a reduced maximum speed of 75mph. February 2021 saw the final pairs of these Class 86s withdrawn from their long term of service. Replacement by former Greater Anglia Class 90s, released from passenger use on the Great Eastern, meant that they could, at last, be stood down in favour of these more powerful steads. The Anglia Railways Class 86/2s, as featured on page 7, shared the East Anglian main line territory with the Freightliner Class 86/6s, though allocated to the Passenger sector and of a higher power output. They were withdrawn from service between 2002 and 2005, the final one being withdrawn that September.

Opposite above: Dawlish, Tuesday, 6 August 2002: Freightliner Class 66/5 66525 in Freightliner livery passes Coryton's Cove with a late morning light engine movement from Exeter Riverside to Moorswater to collect the second half of the cement trip-freight for remarshalling at Exeter Riverside.

The Freightliner green livery looks particularly smart set against the red dune sand sediments forming the sandstone of the South Devon coastline, although erosion has proved an Achilles heel to services using the railway along the sea wall. These cliffs are formed from aeolian (wind-blown) sand which was laid down in a desert in a continental interior in the Permian Period roughly 250 million years ago. As such they are of equal interest to geologists as well as to passengers passing by on this dramatic stretch of railway.

Below: Silverton, Sunday, 31 October 2021: Freightliner Class 66 66517 hauls the 16.35 Exeter St Davids to Westbury civil engineering wagons returning north after engineering work at Exmouth Junction.

This attractive scene viewing the Culm Valley with its rolling hills and colourful Central Devon houses is enhanced by the flood waters of the River Culm. The train was running three hours earlier than its diagrammed time and featured as one of a fleet of such trains taking advantage of the quieter Sunday passenger timetable to make its unhindered passage along this busy stretch of railway. The golden hue of the autumnal colours further provides its own style of narrative to the context of this fine landscape.

Opposite above: Plumley West, Monday, 24 May 2021: Freightliner Class 70 70007 passes Plumley West signal box with the 13.30 Runcorn Folly Lane to Northenden RTS.

A pleasant if anachronistic scene with a semaphore signal and signal box is seen here bypassed with one of the current railway scene's most modern diesels, which reflects the combination of heritage and up-to-date technology in use on the UK railway. The combination of Freightliner green and wrap-around yellow cabs suits this locomotive well, even with its rather awkward grilles. It was on Wednesday, 17 July 2019 that one of these 3,690-horsepower locomotives hauled a trial train with a cargo of aggregate weighing 4,624 tonnes between Merehead, Somerset and Acton. The 'PowerHaul' title given to this design is clearly fully justified.

Opposite below: Plymouth, Sunday, 17 January 2021: Class 66/6 66623 passes with the 08.46 Burngullow Jct. to Westbury empty rail wagons.

It is appropriate on this Sunday morning to observe the two focal churches of Plymouth's Roman Catholic Cathedral of St Mary & St Boniface's and St Peter's Church of England, Wyndham Square. The photographers here are offering their own form of worship and praise as this unusual visitor came their way. The first re-livery and re-branding of a Freightliner locomotive since the acquisition of the company by Genesee & Wyoming in 2015 was revealed as applied to Class 66 66413, which received the orange and black colour scheme of the parent company on the bodyside, along with the new Freightliner logo. Cautiously it is being more widely seen where Freightliner locomotives operate, though there is evidently no rush to extend it to the full fleet. As such, in this guise 66623 offers a rare sight.

Below: Little Langford, Thursday, 5 May 2022: Class 59/2 59204 in recently-liveried Freightliner Genesee & Wyoming colours heads north with the 13.41 Chichester to Merehead Quarry.

Here an idyllic rural scene is exemplified by the ancient Church of St Nicholas situated at the eastern end of the Wylye Valley, characterised by its nave and chancel in twelfth-century style, with a chapel in fourteenth-century Gothic. The tranquil scene's portrait resounds in harmonious rhapsody with its participants, with only a single house nearby for company and the trees clothed in their flourishing spring blossom. The Langfords, Hanging, Steeple and Little, are a picturesque set of villages with traditional Wiltshire cottages and the nearby beautiful Langford Lakes Nature Reserve. The Salisbury to Westbury railway sees regular freight trains alongside frequent passenger services which thread their way through this fine countryside. For the photographer, it is all indeed a rich blessing.

GATWICK EXPRESS

Above: Purley Oaks, Wednesday, 16 April 2003: Gatwick Express Class 460 'Juniper' eight-car electric multiple unit passes with the 16.45 London Victoria to Gatwick Airport. The Driving Motor Lounge First Open is at the rear, and the full train is in Gatwick Express livery.

These intriguing electric multiple units, built by GEC-Alsthom in 1998-99, looked rather like something from a James Bond film set with their distinctive, sloping cab fronts. These earned them an accolade from rail enthusiasts who nicknamed them 'Darth Vaders' after the iconic character in the *Star Wars* series of films. Perhaps this was to distract passengers from the flustered demands of passing through check-in at the airport, or maybe to encourage a view that they too would soon be flying at great height, rather like the spaceships in the films. The reason for the unusual shape of the cab front was somewhat more practical – the coupler was located under the detachable nose cone. Only eight sets were built, replacing Class 73s with dedicated coaching stock.

Opposite above: London Victoria, Monday, 12 March 2018: Southern Class 387/2 Gatwick Express with 387207 at the rear departs for Gatwick with a mid-morning service.

Here is an interesting comparison of liveries, with the South Eastern Class 465 arriving at Victoria as the Gatwick Express Class 387 departs. Each has an attractive style although the Gatwick Express is the most eye-catching. Twenty-seven of the four-car units were ordered by Govia Thameslink Railway. They include more generous luggage space compared to earlier Class 387s, and also feature power points and Wi-Fi.

In the background, many cranes stand sentry- like awaiting their day's use in the long awaited redevelopment of Battersea Power Station. The overall site covers an area of forty-two acres of which eighteen will be public space and six will be used to create a river side park. This 42 acre site accommodates as many as 3,444 new residential homes and vast provision of office and retail space. Provision is also made for shops, bars, restaurants, and cafes.

GB RAILFREIGHT

Below: Silverton, Sunday, 31 October 2021: GBRf Class 66/7 66729 hauls the early-running 12.34 Exeter St Davids to Westbury civil engineering wagons returning north after engineering work at Exmouth Junction.

GB Railfreight has certainly increased its presence over the UK network in recent years, having clearly found a niche for new business and markets, and has consistently needed to increase the size of its fleet to meet the resulting demand. The company has a good rapport with their employees whose satisfaction forms a key aspect of their business acumen. The company has earned a particular interest from the rail enthusiast community, owning several heritage diesel locomotives from Classes 47, 50 and 73, which are deployed in everyday service as well as for the charter sector. Their trains are especially to be seen in the Anglia region, as one of their largest contracts involves moving intermodal trains to and from Felixstowe, and they are significant in their haulage of construction materials to and from quarries in the Peak District. This photograph reminds us that all the freight train operating companies are contracted to haul civil engineers' services.

Above: Devonport, Friday, 12 April 2019: GBRf Class 66/7 66714 hauls GBRf locomotives Class 73 73107, Class 50 50049 and 50007 with the 08.10 Eastleigh to Long Rock for the Penzance depot open day, on Saturday, 13 April.

Here is an illustration exemplifying some of the heritage diesel locomotives operated by GBRf, as mentioned with the previous photograph. It was in January 2019 that GBRf sponsored the repaint of these two Class 50s into GBRf livery, for their use in stock moves. It all looks very smart and suits their long body length particularly well. The Class 50 attachment to West Country expresses was initially less welcome in the south west where they had replaced the highly popular 'Western' Class 52 locomotives, and their reputation for reliability had suffered after working highly demanding schedules on the West Coast main line from which they were displaced after electrification of that route through to Glasgow. Refurbishment and overhaul from the late 1970s to early 1980s all helped to restore their ability to fulfil their potential on the Western Region main line and then on the Waterloo to Exeter route. It was at this time that they received the respected Large Logo blue livery as worn by 50029 *Renown* when seen at Truro in the photograph on page 35.

Opposite above: Hollacombe, Paignton, Saturday, 26 March 2022: UK Rail Tours 'Springtime Hoovering' excursion hauled by GBRf Class 50s 50007 and 50049 passes alongside the South Devon coastline with the 07.35 from London Paddington as they descend towards Paignton.

An advantage for the rail photographers in the South West is that the Devon and Cornwall main line and branch lines offer attractive destinations, fine scenery and plenty of opportunities to hear locomotives climbing the various banks. This train would do just that on the next leg of its journey to Okehampton along the recently reopened branch which has proved highly successful. Given clear spring sunshine the rewarding views can be spectacular, and the passengers on board this train were especially fortuitous.

Below: Ipswich, Friday, 30 May 2008: First GBRf Class 66/7 66718 *Gwyneth Dunwoody* in First GBRf Metronet 'Renewing the Tube' livery/branding in an early afternoon light engine movement from Ipswich stabling point to the station's Up bay briefly, before returning to the stabling point for shunting around its next container train.

Several of the GBRf Class 66/7 locomotives were endowed with this Metronet livery to highlight GBRf's contract with London Underground, where they would assist with moving traffic related to London Underground's huge upgrade programme. The immaculate paintwork indeed carries the London Underground symbol, highlighted by the red swirl – certainly an eye-catching message.

Above: Stowmarket, Friday, 30 May 2008: First GBRf Class 66/7 66718 *Gwyneth Dunwoody* in First GBRf Metronet 'Renewing the Tube' livery/branding passes with an early afternoon container train, operated for Medite Shipping Company (Mondays-Fridays), from Felixstowe to Selby/Doncaster.

Here the same locomotive is seen passing Stowmarket signal box which has been retained beyond modernised resignalling of the area; at the time of writing this 139-year-old Great Eastern Railway signal box no longer operates the signals but it is used to supervise the adjacent manually controlled level crossing barriers by sight (having been re-classified as a gate box). It was during April 2006 that this locomotive was delivered as one of five new low-emission locomotives (numbered 66718-722).

Opposite below: Edinburgh Waverley, Saturday, 5 September 2020: GBRf Class 92 92028 stabled after working the overnight Caledonian Sleepers 23.50 service from London Euston.

In 2019, GBRf introduced the first of their fully refurbished Class 92s for use with the overnight sleeper service from London to Edinburgh and several of GBRf's Class 92s now carry the Caledonian Sleeper midnight teal livery, though not 92028 as yet. The refurbished Class 92s have been fitted with special Dellner couplings, improved communication equipment, and upgraded power to operate the more intensive services offered on this route.

Originally completed in 1996, the Class 92s had previously last operated in service in 2006 before being placed into storage in France. This followed a significant drop in Cross Channel freight using the Channel Tunnel, owing to very high pricing and significantly more competitive rates for lorries. Anticipated duties with continental sleeper services also failed to materialise. These locomotives were technologically advanced for their time, with their ability to draw power from 25 kV AC overhead, on the West Coast Main line, and from the 750 Volts DC third rail network on the Southern Region. They could haul heavy freight trains up the gradients on either side of the Channel Tunnel's base.

Below: Three Arch Bridge, Totnes, Sunday, 26 December 2021: GBRf Class 66/7 66725 passes with the 09.30 Hemerdon to Westbury Down civil engineers' spent ballast train.

Here is a reminder that the Christmas shut down of the UK rail network allows significant civil engineering projects to be undertaken without interruption from passing trains or any requirement to supply replacement buses for suspended passenger train services. On this occasion, the Down main line between Laira Junction and Lipson Junction was being replaced – clearly this would have significantly disrupted all rail traffic in the Plymouth area as it was taking place alongside Laira Depot. As it was, despite none of the usual freight or passenger trains running on Boxing Day, the assembled engineers' trains needed to return to their base with full loads such as this train or with empty track panel wagons, and an interesting procession of these meant an unaccustomed eventful Boxing Day morning for the local rail photographers. Note the seasonal Christmas wreath decorating the cab – a generous gesture by GBRf to recall that it is a special time of year, including for those involved in the Christmas engineering, train driving and signalling who were giving up their holiday for the essential work to take place, ready for families returning to homes or visiting distant members of their family during the Christmas season.

Clapham Junction, Tuesday, 26 May 2009: right, First GB Railfreight Class 66/7 66715 hauls a southbound Metronet engineering train, early afternoon and to its left, London Midland Siemens Desiro UK Class 350/1 350123 passes through with a north-bound ecs (maybe on driver training?).

It is always assumed that the extremely busy Clapham Junction is substantially a passenger train location, with its vast number of platforms, yet there is a surprising amount of freight that passes, especially that which is heading south. It provides an interesting diversion from the plethora of commuter-style trains and express electric multiple units that buzz around like bees around a nest, awaiting their turn to deliver the honey, or should we say passengers – or even, as here, the civil engineering load. One can only speculate how many passengers, or customers in today's parlance, pass over the distinctive footbridge each rush hour.

GNER (GREAT NORTH EASTERN RAILWAY)

Grantham, Tuesday, 27 May 1997: GNER Class 91 91031 *Sir Henry Royce* with the 16.05 Leeds to London King's Cross.

This full set of locomotive and coaches in GNER livery certainly exudes a business-like appearance. GNER's trains were painted dark blue – the same colour as the Venice-Simplon Orient Express European luxury train operation which was also owned by GNER's parent company Sea Containers, a transport and freight-container company, and this was offset by a red stripe. Some coaching sets carried the GNER legend in gold lettering, and in the lower middle of the carriages was applied the GNER's own 'crest' which featured the Lion Rampant of Scotland (on the left) and the Lion Passant which represented England (on the right), Thistles (the flower of Scotland) and Tudor roses (the flower of England) at top and bottom. This was to commemorate the fact that on London to Edinburgh services, these trains ran on the same route as that taken by the celebrated *Flying Scotsman*.

It is reassuring to note that the Class 91s under LNER ownership have earned extended service life as the company has retained seven Mk 4 coaching sets along with ten class 91s to ensure, initially, that the enhanced 2021 winter timetable could be fulfilled, even if restricted to services to Leeds. The plan is to keep them on lease until at least December 2023.

Edinburgh Waverley, Thursday, 1 June 2000: GNER livery Class 90 90024 stabled, and GNER livery HST with power car 43038 at rear departing with the 14.00 ex-London King's Cross to Aberdeen.

Electrification of Edinburgh Waverley for the Class 91s to operate through trains from London King's Cross meant that photographers would find their favoured viewpoints at Princes Gardens for capturing the busy rail scene on camera compromised by the accompanying masts and wiring. With the mediaeval old town and castle glowering over the deep cutting in which Waverley is built, sunlight is an essential element to lightening the scene – this mid-spring showery day suggests it beholds a passing presence at times. Yet in many ways the environment has not changed, for BR's impressive roaring Deltics or the LNER's A2 and A4 magnificent hissing Pacifics needed similarly to exert their presence in these historic surroundings. In today's contemporary scene, quiet Azumas and suburban electric multiple units come and go almost unnoticed, with only their warning hoots audible as they enter the tunnels (either side of the station) to disturb the throngs of tourists in Princes Street, high above the action. That here is a key rail artery which strikes through the centre of Scotland's capital city, in parallel with its most famous shopping street, and in deference to the royal castle and ancient fortifications above it, all offers an interesting commentary on the interaction of landscape, architecture and railway transport.

Hadley Wood, Saturday, 28 September 2002: Class 373 'Regional Eurostar' 14-carriage set 3304 in GNER livery passes with the 14.30 service from London King's Cross to Leeds. Hadley Wood North Tunnel is in the background.

The 'Regional Eurostar' was a planned train service from Paris to Brussels and locations in the United Kingdom beyond just the Capital. It was originally planned to use a fleet of seven North of London 14-coach Class 373/3 train sets from London to Manchester via Birmingham and to Glasgow via Newcastle.

However, very long journey times compared to air travel deemed these operations unviable, for at the same time there had been a huge expansion of low-cost airlines during the 1990s offering competitive rates and journey times from various regional airports to Paris. Due to a low forecast of expected passenger numbers on inter-capital train services, by 1998 this was considered uneconomical to develop and the scheme was quietly dropped. Three of these redundant sets were then leased by GNER for a short while to increase capacity. From 12 December 2005, these Regional Eurostar sets were withdrawn from these services and returned to European Passenger Services. They did see further use in France under the ownership of SNCF.

BRITAIN'S CHANGING TRAIN LIVERIES • 115

GREAT WESTERN

Didcot Railway Centre, Sunday, 30 July 2000: left, Collett design GWR Class 4073 'Castle' 4-6-0 4079 *Pendennis Castle* , and right Cardiff Railway 0-4-0ST 1338.

The famed Great Western 'Castle' Class held sway hauling passenger express trains through the height of the Great Western era and from 1948 during the early British Railways era. They traversed a variety of landscapes offered by the lines to the Devon and Cornish holiday resorts, and also through the industrial hearts of South Wales and the West Midlands. One of their pinnacles of achievement was the world's fastest scheduled service delivered by the 'Cheltenham Flyer' which during the 1920s and 1930s established an impressive journey time of one hour ten minutes for the seventy-seven miles.

Cardiff Railway 1338, designed by Kitson and built in 1898, offers an interesting contrast. Notably built without a coal bunker, it would have spent much time pottering around the docks and colliery sidings served by the Cardiff Railway, and in GWR ownership at Bridgwater docks, Somerset. With no such claim to fame as its larger compatriot above, it served a distinct if unglamorous purpose and its longevity enabled it to survive into preservation, in which it receives the interest and attention that its hard work deserves.

GREAT WESTERN RAILWAY

Umberleigh, Wednesday, 4 November 2020: A Class 158 departs with the 11.35 from Barnstaple to St James Park.

These Class 158 trains brought a vastly improved quality of journey to the Barnstaple branch, which had only recently previously seen extensive use of Pacers and Class 150s. Many passengers travel the full length of the line, alongside a healthy contingent commuting to and from Crediton, and the length of such at one hour and ten minutes to Exeter Central surely justified their deployment. These were cascaded from Portsmouth to Cardiff services once adequate Class 165 and 166 Turbo units were available for use on these, displaced by new electric multiple units provided for London Paddington to Reading, Newbury and Didcot services. Grazing sheep often occupy the field in the foreground and are a significant aspect of the region's farming. A local farmer once told me exactly where the resident adders sheltered in the heat of the afternoon in his outbuildings!

Opposite above: Kingford, Wednesday, 4 November 2020: Class 158 158749 passes with the 13.35 from Barnstaple to St James Park.

These trains unusually, and only for about a couple of seasons, terminated and turned around at St James Park which primarily served the football stadium which is the home of Exeter City FC. It is interesting to see that this is a single two-car unit whereas a couple of units were often provided even for off-peak mid-day services, as such occurred during the peak of the Covid pandemic and facilitated social distancing on the later busier services. At the date of this picture, the virus was starting to surge again before a second lockdown was needed to restrict its spread, after which further Covid-19 variants emerged.

Opposite below: Yeoford, 25 November 2021: Class 158 158798 calls at the Up platform with the 11.35 Barnstaple to Exeter Central.

Some of the shrubbery on the disused Down platform has been removed, but although the line serving it has seen daily use since the relaunch on 20 November 2021 of the two-hourly Okehampton services, hourly in the summer timetable, there are no plans yet for the Okehampton services to call there – and as the Okehampton and Barnstaple lines are segregated after Crediton, the Barnstaple trains can't call there either as there is no physical connection to this Down line until just west of Crediton. The fine display of autumn trees' gold and red colours surround the line in the distance – no doubt shedding their leaves in abundance and threatening likely wheel slip for passing trains.

Below: Polbathic Bridge, near St Germans, Sunday, 6 December 2020: A 9-car Class 800 ascends towards Trerulefoot with the 09.35 London Paddington to Penzance.

The Great Western Railway green livery applied to the Class 800 InterCity Express fleet has not always made for easy photography, being somewhat darker than the original colour it seeks to emulate. However it fits comfortably into the pastel of nature's winter greens seen here contrasting with the approaching darker shadows that will soon envelope the passing trains along this section of the Cornish main line. Dartmoor looms in the background, looking resonant with its own tapestry of autumnal gold.

Above: Silverton, Sunday, 31 October 2021: Great Western Railway Class 800/3 IET 800321 leads the 10.18 Penzance to London Paddington.

Here is a highly visible reminder of the pandemic times that held sway during the years 2020 to 2021. Great Western Railway has applied artwork in the form of giant face coverings to either end of one of its high-speed Intercity Express Trains. The 'masked' IET re-entered service on 15 June 2020, on the same day that it became mandatory to wear a face covering on public transport as part of the easement on lockdown restrictions. The intention was to reinforce the message about wearing a face covering when travelling on the trains in order to help keep passengers on board safe. Certainly, intending passengers on this train wouldn't need to be reminded, as they'd see the face mask as it arrived. Such a message needed to be repeated in the autumn of 2021 with the upsurge of new cases, especially from the 'Omicron' variant.

Opposite above: Trerulefoot, Friday, 2 April 2021: 'Castle' Class HST set with 43041 *St Catherine's Castle* at the rear, passes by with the 13.50 Penzance to Plymouth.

The Great Western Railway green livery worn by the IETs and "Castle" Class HSTs stands out well against nature's green backdrop, especially when enhanced by the red-backed cast nameplates and the white GWR insignia as seen here. These shortened form HSTs have proved a great success, replacing previously-allocated Sprinters suited to more suburban services while providing the same high quality ride for regional travel in the West Country that was customary to regular passengers travelling on the 'original' long distance HSTs to and from London. Initial plans for eleven sets were increased to fourteen, covering twelve diagrams per day, including Penzance to Cardiff via Weston-Super-Mare, and make good use of trains that, while starting to show their age, would only have otherwise been stored out of use or scrapped. The application of West Country castle names helps passengers further identify with them within the travel area and builds a local appeal of these trains.

Below: Forder Viaduct, Friday, 14 January 2022: Great Western 'Castle' Class HST crosses with the 13.43 Plymouth to Penzance.

The low winter sunlight enhances the reflections in the calm high tide waters of Latchbrook Leat (an inlet off the Lynher River estuary). The Great Western green livery corresponds with the green of the grass where caressed by gentle shadows in the field behind the train, accompanied by the red nameplate of 43170 *Chepstow Castle* adding an appropriate splash of colour. Nature frames the trainset within its own winter hues and the scene represents Cornwall's pastoral valleys at their best.

Above: Laira Embankment, 14 April 2020: Class 57 57603 *Tintagel Castle* passes with empty Sleeper coaches working from Reading TCD to Penzance.

This train would normally pass Plymouth in the hours of darkness, except in mid-summer on its Down journey, when it is just light enough to capture on camera en route to Penzance. On the illustrated occasion, this was a swap of Sleeper stock that occurred during the lockdown of the first wave of the Covid pandemic. It passes the high tide of the Plym estuary in pleasant spring sunshine; it was somewhat ironic that some of the finest spells of spring weather for many years occurred during the lockdown underway at that time. The road in the background was virtually empty whereas it is normally constantly busy at this time of day.

Opposite above: Plymouth, Wednesday, 13 October 2021: 'Castle' Class HST set on a late afternoon westbound service with power car 43093 at the rear, carrying its *Old Oak Common HST Depot 1976-2018* commemorative nameplate.

This highly evocative image, referred to as 'Legends of the Great Western' in special vinyl graphic on the side of the power car, shows the various forms of motive power that were familiar sights when based at Old Oak Common including 'Castles', 'Westerns', 'Hymeks' and 'Warships'. The ethereal atmosphere implies a reminiscence recalling 'Ghosts of Times Past' which is effective and distinctive – a worthy tribute to this important depot.

GREAT WESTERN TRAINS

Below: Forder Viaduct, Friday, 23 July 1999: First Great Western HST in Great Western Trains Swallow livery crosses with the 14.32 London Paddington to Penzance.

This dark green and ivory 'Great Western Merlin' colour scheme was worn by HSTs operating into the West Country beyond the rebranding of the Great Western Trains franchise as 'First Great Western' by the First Group in December 1998. It forms an attractive livery along with the Great Western green, white and gold stripe displayed by the coaching stock, and both liveries correspond well with the natural greens of the Cornish countryside.

Devonport, Friday, 25 June 1999: Great Western Trains Swallow livery Class 47/4 47830 with the 14.32 FO London Paddington, 18.20 Plymouth to Penzance, hauling MkIIF set of carriages substituting for an unavailable HST.

A Great Western Trains locomotive and hauled set of InterCity carriages, both now under First Group ownership as explained above, provides an interesting if unusual comparison to the usual HSTs along the Great Western railway from London to and from Penzance as illustrated in the previous picture. The cutting allows a fine resonance of sound from the accelerating green Class 47, and the mid-summer early evening light helps illuminate the scene in which west-bound trains would otherwise be in shadow.

HEATHROW EXPRESS

London Paddington, Tuesday, 3 April 2007: left and centre, Heathrow Express Class 332 electric multiple units 332004 and 005; right, First Great Western 'Adelante' Class 180 180103.

The Royal Bank of Scotland Group (RBS) advertising proved an attractive colour on these smart units, although one does wonder who or what is supposed to 'make it happen' – seen on the left hand carriage – a message for the first class businessmen who wheel and deal in finance and politics maybe, and who are using the train to connect to their flight? It seems a less applicable message to the tourists using the train when heading away from London on a departing flight from Heathrow, and even less so to casual observers on the platform. Certainly, the message is that the Spanish train construction company CAF (Grupo CAF, 'Construction & Other Railway Services') can build smart and comfortable units. Or maybe it refers to Heathrow Express which at the time explained on their website that their trains were the fastest way between London Paddington and Heathrow Central, taking just 15 minutes to Terminals 2 and 3, and 6 minutes more to Terminal 5. The 'Heathrow Express' Class 332 fleet was finally withdrawn in December 2020, replaced by Class 387 electric units.

London Paddington, Tuesday, 3 April 2007: 'Heathrow Express' Class 332 electric multiple units 332005 and 011, early evening.

At the date of this photograph, the overhead electrification only extended to Heathrow, and this is a remarkably exhaust-free scene more likely to occur in the latter part of the second decade from when Great Western Railway Class 800 IETs have departed silently under the wires to Reading and beyond; in fact the whole station can now be full of quietly awaiting electric trains and the era of diesel engine trains at Paddington is nearly entirely history. The clean air here enables a view of the marvellous trainshed that Isambard Kingdom Brunel and Matthew Digby Wyatt designed. Wyatt had been involved with the design of the Crystal Palace (opened 1851) and his architectural features no doubt influenced some of the characteristics of Paddington, especially in the use of wrought iron and glass in the three-span roof. It is to be justifiably compared with the great Norman cathedrals in its nave-like high arches and pillars extending upwards, with fan-like iron tracery that reaches towards its vaulted and partly clad roof. In such a way it also recalls the splendour and synchronous harmony of London St Pancras trainshed. Drawing on the ecclesiastical comparison, it is as if we look towards its transepts at the far end Lawn, more recently extended to a double height structure of glass and concrete at the station's south end. Once the stationmaster's garden, this area became a public concourse in 1933. Just as one might sit inside and admire the mediaeval cathedral's vast spacious interiors and intricate stonework so designed to raise the worshippers' eyes to the Heavens, so also might one sit in the Lawn and look outwards on this masterpiece in adulation and adoration.

HIGHLAND RAILWAY

Friday, 17 September 2021, Inverness: Highland Railway Jones Goods 4-6-0.

Pub signs illustrating trains vary in accuracy concerning the subject they endeavour to portray both in livery and class of locomotive; here is an example of one that is certainly admirable. Some railway artists even specialise in painting pub signs for hostelries in their localities. This example can be seen at a pub just around the corner from Inverness station.

This sign appears to be an effort to capture both in authentic livery and design detail a Highland Railway Jones Goods 4-6-0. Built by Sharp, Stewart & Co. in Glasgow, it was one of fifteen referred to as the 'Big Goods' class; they were adapted for the severe curvature of the Highland main line. Jones' design was relatively unchanged by the LMS when the locomotives passed into their ownership, thus implying a creditable quality of build.

There seems to be some dispute as to what the livery colour actually is. As a form of green as used by the Highland Railway from at least the 1870s until c.1900, it was an olive green made from chrome yellow and carbon black (or lamp black) pigments. It is likely the lighter colour worn by the Jones Goods was also an olive green with more yellow than the dark olive border colour.

In 1865, William Stroudley moved to Inverness as locomotive superintendent of the Highland Railway, becoming their chief mechanical engineer the following year. One of the changes to the locomotives that he introduced in his time at Inverness was a new livery, one of his own devising, to be called 'Improved Engine Green'. The problem was that Improved Engine Green wasn't green. It has been compared with gamboge (a dark mustard yellow pigment), or a golden yellow ochre.

After withdrawal and preservation, Jones Goods 103 was first restored by the LMS to the colour shown in the sign, Stroudley yellow, which colour it wore for a short time after being built. This colour was disputed by enthusiasts as to its accuracy as Highland Railway colour, but it is likely they matched paint to that which would have still been visible in the layers of paint on the locomotive.

HUNSLET-BARCLAY

Menheniot, Saturday, 7 April 1990: Class 20/9 Hunslet-Barclay owned 20901 *Nancy* with the east-bound spraying Chipman's Weed-Killing train, heading for Keyham.

This private operator with its own silver livery brought additional variety to the Nineties railway scene with the Chipmans Weed-Killing Train trundling the rails of the South West. The growth of vegetation on preserved railways which did not reopen during the initial pandemic year made some of the branches look as if the days of Beeching had returned, so quickly did they take on a desolate and deserted appearance. This, of course, was later dealt with by cutting-back work parties who found themselves with a vastly increased workload. Fortunately, with their hard work and the return to use of the disused rails by timetabled trains, many regained their familiar tidy appearance.

INTERCITY

Tavistock Junction, Wednesday, 31 October 1990: Class 47/4 47840 accelerates with the 12.40 Penzance to London Paddington.

   The driver gives a cheerful wave to the permanent way gang, for without them his train would no doubt face a rough ride over inadequately maintained track. The railway industry is in some respects rather like a large family, each aware of the needs of their fellow co-workers, whether their roles are working on the tracks or as customer hosts on the trains, or in despatching trains from busy platforms.

   The InterCity brand needed a smart livery and, kept clean, it presented an image of a corporate business efficiently meeting the needs of business as well as leisure travellers.

Opposite above: Waterside, Saturday, 28 August 2021: Class 47/4 47828 threads its way along the Dartmouth Steam Railway with the return 17.25 Kingswear to High Wycombe 'Dartmouth Royal Regatta Statesman'.

There are usually some additional trains operated along this preserved line for the busy Dartmouth Regatta weekend, using the preserved Railway's home fleet of diesels, and occasionally this is supplemented by main line charters, such as seen here against the attractive backdrop of Churston Cove in marvellous August bank holiday summer sunshine. The immaculate paintwork of this Locomotive Services Class 47 is matched by the equally superb Statesman Rail Pullman coaching stock livery and is a credit to the operators and owners of these fine trains. It's almost unfortunate that the passengers on board don't quite share the same view of their fine steed to enhance their own travel experience.

Opposite below: Near Foley Park, Severn Valley Railway, Thursday, 18 May 2017: Class 50 50031 *Hood* in InterCity livery descends the bank with the 14.13 Kidderminster to Bewdley.

Wearing a fictitious livery, it is an interesting reflection on a livery that might have been applied to the Class 50 fleet. It suits the long locomotive body and has proved popular with photographers and 'haulage' enthusiasts. The historic coaches in their chocolate and cream don't quite blend with this comparatively modern diesel, but that's a small quibble – they are very appropriate for appearing along with the Severn Valley Railway's GWR steam locomotives which on every day during the running season ply the scenic line dovetailing the River Severn. Purists need to be ready to compromise.

Below: London Paddington, Friday, 20 May 2016: Class 43 power car 43002, the first production HST power car, in vinyl wrap of original HST blue/yellow/grey commemorating trainset 253 001 and given the name *Sir Kenneth Grange* to commemorate the man who created the iconic HST design.

This was named at Bristol St Philips Marsh depot at its open day, on 2 May 2016, to celebrate 40 years since the introduction of the Class to British Rail's Western Region. I travelled on the train illustrated to London without realising this iconic power car was on the rear until I noticed various photographers en route clearly photographing the rear power car of the train from Plymouth, and on investigation at Paddington I realised exactly what was causing the interest on an otherwise rather dull morning. The power car remained in this special livery until its withdrawal in 2019, and proved a favourite subject for photographers, especially in the South West.

Ives Plantation near Haworth, Keighley and Worth Valley Railway, Saturday, 4 May 2019: Prototype HST power car 41001 is seen in transit behind DRS Class 88 88009 on the 13.15 Keighley to Oxenhope.

This now unique Prototype HST power car was built in 1972 with its companion 41002 at British Rail Engineering Limited in Crewe, both of which preceded production power car 43002 illustrated in the previous photograph. This pair earned their fame when they travelled at a speed of 143.2 mph (around Northallerton on the East Coast Main Line) which justifiably gave the HST the honour of the world speed record for diesel traction. Belonging to the National Collection and after many years on display at the York National Railway Museum (NRM), it has been operating at the Great Central Nottingham heritage railway after being returned to operating condition in conjunction with the 125 Group. It now resides back at the NRM situated close to other equally iconic speed-breaking locomotives.

INDUSTRIAL

Buckfastleigh, South Devon Railway, Monday, 22 April 2019: Andrew Barclay 0-4-0ST No.1219 *Caledonia Works*.

Built in 1910 at the Andrew Barclay Caledonia Works in Kilmarnock, this locomotive worked in Scotland for Stewart & Lloyd Ltd at the Clydedale Works in Mossend. In preservation it was often seen at Washford on the West Somerset Railway, performing similar shunting duties as seen here, all usually associated with the Somerset and Dorset Railway Trust. At Buckfastleigh it was involved in a display event forming part of the South Devon Railway's 50th Anniversary Gala, This locomotive provided a fascinating demonstration shunting a small characteristic set of freight wagons to illustrate aspects of branch line freight. It stayed around the Buckfastleigh site and emerged from the sidings in between the busy schedule of special trains arriving and departing during this anniversary.

LAMBTON, HETTON & JOICEY COLLIERY COMPANY (LH&JC)

Water Ark, North Yorkshire Moors Railway, Friday, 24 September 2021: LH&JC 0-6-2T No.29 descends towards Grosmont with a demonstration freight train.

The variety of colours in this train consist recalls the days of private owner company wagons which with their specific liveries helped identify wagons belonging to each owners' fleet. The coal wagons are indeed highly appropriate for their haulage behind this Robert Stephenson & Hawthorn built locomotive. Rather like some of the London, Tilbury and Southend Railway's 4-4-2T 'Tilbury Tanks', this locomotive was delivered to its owners in 1909. However, rather than hauling suburban commuters, this powerful tank engine was used to haul heavy coal trains in the north eastern landscape. It would climb the steep gradients up to the County Durham collieries before descending with its loads to the staithes at Sunderland which served boats for onward shipment. The railways formed a crucial part of the logistics that served this important trade.

LOADHAUL

Didcot, Sunday, 30 July 2000 : Class 60 60008 *Gypsum Queen II* in Loadhaul livery, with a Civil Engineers' grey Class 08 on the left.

Didcot A power station, as fuelled by coal and oil, once seemed a permanent fixture on the Oxfordshire landscape – but now the cooling towers have been demolished and, nominated Didcot B, it is now an efficient combined cycle gas power plant powered by natural gas.

It was in the mid-1990s that British Rail decided to concentrate its freight operations in three 'shadow freight' companies. To achieve this BR divided the country into three regions, with Loadhaul based in the north-east. Like Mainline, the company decided to repaint their fleet of allocated locomotives in this eye-catching black and orange colour scheme. The Class 60s once looked doomed to extinction during the early part of the first decade of the new millennium, with up to three quarters of the fleet out of service, but their fortunes changed and they continue to haul heavy freight – often seen usually working with oil tankers, steel and stone traffic.

LONDON, BRIGHTON AND SOUTH COAST RAILWAY (LBSCR)

Opposite above and below: Corfe Common, Swanage Railway, Sunday, 12 September 2010: Leading locomotive LBSCR 0-6-0T Class A1X 'Terrier', 32662 *Martello*; rear locomotive, GWR 0-6-2T 5600 Class 6695 push/pull locomotives with the 14.50 Norden to Harman's Cross.

It may be here on LSWR territory, but 32662 *Martello* looks especially at home on this branch line, even if its diminutive size is a little daunted by Corfe Castle's dominant silhouette. Its Marsh umber blends in well with the relatively gentle Purbeck Hills countryside and it seems to be enjoying a new lease of life after its days hauling London commuter trains. These engines could manage a lengthy 12 coaches on demanding workings requiring acceleration away from regular stops at busy suburban platforms. Eventually, the Class found themselves in less demanding work such as shunting or on light goods trains. *Martello* saw service on the Hayling Island branch from around the mid-1920s until it transferred to the Newhaven Harbour Company in 1955. It is truly remarkable to find such a locomotive built in 1875 still in occasional service in its preservation life and holding immense respect among the steam enthusiast fraternity.

Below: Sheffield Park, Bluebell Railway, Tuesday, 4 August 1998: LBSCR 0-6-0T Class A1X 'Terrier', 55 *Stepney*.

Here we see again (as referred to in the above notes for Highland Railway Jones Goods 4-6-0 on page 127) Stroudley's 'Improved Engine Green' livery which appears less green and more golden yellow ochre. Built in the same year as *Martello* (1875), this locomotive became an early example of preservation on the Bluebell which helped to show their importance, and explains their appeal to the steam preservation movement. They became well known as 'Terriers' thanks to their distinctive exhaust beat 'bark'. They could be seen hauling commuter services in London and later worked on the Sussex branch lines such as the Bluebell line, where they lasted longer than many pre-grouping tank engines. They earned fame for their use on the Hayling Island line where the weight restriction on the bridge to the island meant such light engines (at 28 tons) were necessary. Ten members of the class have been acquired for preservation.

LONDON MIDLAND AND SCOTTISH (LMS) MAROON

Manor Road Station, Sunday, 6 April 1986: Preserved Class 502 electric multiple unit M29896 and M28361, preserved by the NRM and on loan to Southport Steamport, is seen providing short runs to and from Hoylake as part of the Mersey Railway Centenary.

In the mid-1930s the LMS changed their design of suburban electric trains. Instead of individual carriage compartments they featured an open saloon layout, with rows of seats either side of a central aisle, with two pairs of double power-operated sliding doors on each side of the car that opened into a wide entrance lobby. These proved well suited for the many third rail electric lines radiating from Liverpool Exchange. Class 502 sets, such as here illustrated, first received the standard LMS maroon red. Post-nationalisation they were repainted in light malachite green and they eventually received standard BR dark green for EMUs. They later gained yellow warning panels on their cab fronts. I especially recollect these passing through Hightown, my local station, and through Hall Road station from the stabling sidings, en route for use in the afternoon rush hour. This was when the units were being repainted into plain Rail Blue, retaining the small yellow warning panel. This 2-car set, formed of motor car 28361 and driving trailer 29896, was preserved by the National Railway Museum. It was placed on extended loan to the Steamport railway centre at Southport. In 1986 British Rail celebrated the 100th anniversary of the Mersey Railway. Steamport was delighted to offer use of this Class 502 as part of the celebrations, and thus it operated a special shuttle between Birkenhead North and Hoylake, so making the Class 502 the first privately-restored EMU to work a revenue-earning train on the BR network.

LONDON NORTH EASTERN RAILWAY

Berwick-upon-Tweed, Friday, 4 September 2020: Class 800 'Azuma' IET crosses the Royal Border Bridge with the 13.30 London King's Cross to Edinburgh service.

The old castle fortifications, seen on the left, date from the thirteenth century and culminated in the great artillery ramparts begun in 1558, which survive largely intact and make Berwick one of the most important fortified towns of Europe. Their heritage salutes one of the most technically advanced types of train on Britain's railway network, here seen crossing the most northerly arches of this 28-arch viaduct which equally required substantial engineering innovation during its own time of construction.

Robert Stephenson was the railway's engineer, though most of the line engineering was undertaken by Thomas Harrison under Stephenson's supervision. It is interesting that three very different types of engineering combine here to represent their distinct pinnacle of engineering excellence and fortitude, and each deserves its own timely accolade.

Dalmeny, Friday, 4 September 2020: Class 801 'Azuma' IET heads south and away from the south portal of the Forth Bridge with the 07.55 Inverness to London King's Cross, diverted from its usual route as a result of the Union Canal bursting its banks and flooding the line near Polmont on the route towards Falkirk and Stirling.

The sleek lines of the Forth Bridge are echoed by the sleek lines of the 'Azuma', all helped by the distinctive grey and white swirl and flowing red band on the side of the leading driving cab. It's certainly an impressive futuristic image that is demonstrated in this train design. Similar European High Speed electric trains mirror the desire to convey a sense of speed through their glossy arrow-like protruding train cab nose designs first seen in the Japanese Bullet Trains. This style is typified by German Railways' ICE3s, Trenitalia's Frecciarossa (*Red Arrow*) ETR 1000s and Spain's Alta Velocidad Española (AVE) Talgo 350 HSR trains, not forgetting SNCF's trend setting TGVs which held the World Rail Speed record (357 miles an hour) in April 2007. Of course, the Italian's ETR 3000 *Settebello* exclusive 1st class express train that ran from 1953, which ran between Milan and Rome, reflected the desire to impress with similar dynamic train designs. Likewise, Germany's 1930s *Fliegender Hamburger* (Flying Hamburger) which reached a maximum speed of 100 miles per hour, with an average speed of 77·4 miles per hour from Berlin to Hamburg. The UK's pre-war LNER streamlined locomotives and coaching stock forming the *Silver Jubilee* and *Coronation Scot* and the LMS competitive *Coronation Scot* all emphasised a common message: 'It's Quicker By Rail' as the LNER publicity posters emphasised.

London King's Cross, Wednesday, 17 June 2020: A line up of Class 800 'Azuma' London North Eastern Railway IET trains.

By the time of this photograph, the 'Azuma' revolution had swiftly established this new fleet of IET trains in scheduled use on the East Coast main line, and a standard image such as this presented a considerable change to that of the Class 91s which had ruled the roost for many years previously. To operate bi-mode trains that can extend beyond the wires to Harrogate or Aberdeen is quite an advance in terms of the British railway scene, with similar Great Western Railway units extending beyond Newbury to the West Country, although SNCF have used bi-mode trains in service for over a decade. An additional advantage for the bi-mode version of these trains is that they can operate away from overhead wires when engineering closes part of the East Coast route and diversion is required, for example via Lincoln or via Carlisle, the latter enabling a very pleasant if leisurely trip over the Hadrian's Wall line as it passes close to many attractive former Roman towns and villages, and skirts the edge of the scenic Northumberland National Park. The time penalty is very worthwhile. I have personally also benefited from such when wires had been pulled down by a recalcitrant pantograph north of Biggleswade and enjoyed a re-routing northwards via Cambridge, Ely and March, thus giving an intriguing journey by one of the very new trains crossing heritage- era rural gated crossings providing farm access to fertile East Anglian fields.

As for the Class 91s, at the time of writing LNER will be retaining on lease, until at least December 2023, seven Mk 4 sets with ten Class 91s to ensure that the enhanced 2021 winter timetable and ensuing timetables can be fulfilled. They will be used on services to Leeds but no further north as the 'thunderbird' rescue Class 67 locomotives have been removed from Edinburgh.

LONDON OVERGROUND

Highbury and Islington, Saturday, 18 June 2011: London Overground Class 378 electric multiple units; right: 378149 with an east-bound departure mid-afternoon, left: 378139 with a westbound mid-afternoon service for Clapham Junction, both in London Overground livery.

These smart new trains had appeared on services which had been recently extended from Dalston Junction to New Cross Gate and New Cross from 27 April 2011 on weekdays and from 15 May at weekends. Also in May 2011, services were extended from Dalston Junction to Highbury and Islington. This meant that full services were restored to the East London Line, after a £1 billion upgrade. Their longitudinal seating means there are fewer seats than on trains with conventional seating but there is significant space for standees, with seat perches generously spread throughout the train, and this therefore enables them to carry a high capacity, which is especially useful at busy times. They have especially contributed to the appeal of the London Overground System which continues to prove very popular for providing frequent useful connections linking 23 of London's 33 boroughs. London Overground is part of the National Rail network, run as a rail franchise by the train operating company London Overground Rail Operations Ltd, but the contracting authority is Transport for London (TfL) rather than central government.

LONDON TRANSPORT (LT)/TRANSPORT FOR LONDON (TFL)

London, North Ealing Station, Saturday, 22 March 1997: Piccadilly line stock operating a service to Uxbridge, in 'United Airlines' livery.

United Airlines operates a large domestic and international route network spanning cities across the USA. Presuming the power of advertising on a London Transport tube train is going to be seen by potentially hundreds of thousands of Tube passengers, it must be worth the cost of such sponsorship. It was certainly unusual to see such advertising adorning the full cab and sides of this stock. It seems to be a quiet part of the day, judging by the number of passengers available to view such a promotion. Once passengers are inside the train, of course, the advert will no longer be visible to them – always a disadvantage of exterior adverts – but buses frequently carry exterior advertising and their promoters must see the financial benefits of such. This location is also a reminder that deep level tube trains also run above ground – not a fact appreciated by all who visit London and use the central zones only.

BRITAIN'S CHANGING TRAIN LIVERIES • 143

Sheringham, North Norfolk Railway, Thursday, 13 June 2019: Class 20 20227 *Sherlock Holmes*, in London Transport Metropolitan maroon livery, arrives with the 10.35 from Holt.

This last-built Class 20 locomotive has worked extensively on the London Underground network, including during the 'Steam on the Met' events in the late 1990s and in 2000 and has been repainted in London Transport livery by its owners – the Class 20 Locomotive Society – in recognition of this. The famed detective would have needed some discernment to find the nameplate. He might also have been intrigued to see a locomotive bearing these colours on a preserved railway that closely follows the North Norfolk coast. That, of course, was all part of the attraction of the locomotive's visit to the railway – and it does look impressive alongside the platform canopy which has in recent years been faithfully restored in its original style.

High Street Kensington, Friday, 20 May 2016: TfL 'S7' train departs with a mid-afternoon District line service to Wimbledon.

The 'S' type stock which has during recent years displaced older trains on the Circle, District, Hammersmith & City and Metropolitan lines has brought a much improved travel experience for commuters and tourists alike. Importantly, they are equipped with air conditioning, a feature much appreciated – for when travelling in the older trains during very warm weather, temperatures inside the trains became unbearably hot as a result of a combination of body heat and heat from the train's motors. Equally helpful is the spacious interior which, although with limited seats, allows movement within the full length of the train. Passengers can move to less crowded areas within the carriages and this helps to relieve congestion, especially in sections of carriages which stop nearer platform exits and entrances (a particular problem in the older trains, especially in the rush hour). They are also provided with selective door operation for use in stations where platforms are shorter than the length of the trains. The white paint of the station canopies relieves some of the surrounding darker stained brickwork, while the platform level furniture and wire piping running below there and rather untidily along the cutting walls, along with the third and fourth rails and the crossover beyond the platforms, all contributes an integral identity to this surface level station in the heart of London.

Turnham Green, Monday, 14 March 2016: TfL 1973 stock Piccadilly line train bound for Cockfosters.

After enjoying its escape from the depths of the low level tube on its outward journey, this tube train returns towards the tunnels that will take it far below the bustling streets in the evening rush hour and eventually to Cockfosters on the far north side of the city. The sunset bids it farewell – for when it makes its next journey through here, the darkness of a cool early spring night will have descended. The cheerful red glow of sunset pays tribute to the predominantly red driver's cab and silhouettes the trees as if conveying a false sense of the rural nature of this inner suburban location. For those with time to spare, there is a pub close by which offers a convivial atmosphere, decent real ale and even a small library of books with which to divert the visiting traveller's attention from their later lengthy train journey home, for they are just as equally keen to escape the inevitable grasp of the metropolis which may be echoed by the tube train's escape from the perpetual darkness of the underground tube lines. Delivery of 94 New Tube for London trains to the Piccadilly line is scheduled for 2023, with trains to enter service in 2024 after testing.

MAINLINE BLUE

Keighley, Saturday, 26 April 2003: Class 60 60011 in Mainline Blue livery with a northbound empty gypsum train from Eggborough Power Station to Carlisle, passing at about midday.

Loadhaul, Mainline Freight and Transrail were formed in 1994, when British Rail decided to concentrate its freight operations in three 'shadow freight' companies. To achieve this, BR divided the country into three regions, with Mainline in charge of freight logistics operations to the south and east, extending from South Yorkshire to Kent. The livery was formally described as aircraft blue with a silver bodyside stripe. It was most noteworthy as seen on Class 33, 37, 58 and 60 locomotives, with 60011 one of just three Class 60s to make it into Mainline Blue livery. A small number of Class 73s, closely associated with the Southern Region, also received the livery. A large rolling wheels logo was applied to the sides. The heavy weight of this Class 60 locomotive at 129-131 tons would not be too welcome on the neighbouring Keighley and Worth Valley Railway, although Class 50 locomotives have appeared at the railway's diesel galas and their 115 ton weight has journeyed the full length of the line without problems.

Above: Woking, Sunday, 22 October 1995: Class 37s stabled, left, 37/0 37074 in Mainline Blue livery and right, Class 37/3 37375 in Civil Engineer's livery.

This Mainline Class 37 carries a fresh and pristine coat of the paint in the early days of this freight operator and looks proud to be on display. There was a Mainline two-tone grey livery version applied to many of the Class 58s and some Class 60s on which just the rolling wheels logo was applied, but this was certainly less than spectacular. Mainline Blue made a welcome difference to the usual colours around the area served and was popular with both enthusiasts and photographers.

MIDLAND MAINLINE

Opposite above: Ely, Wednesday, 28 May 2008: Class 170/1 2-car Turbostar passes near Ely Cathedral with an early afternoon service to Leicester and Birmingham from Stansted Airport.

This is one of the former Central Trains fleet and new to Midland Mainline. It was transferred to Central Trains in 2004 and to CrossCountry in late 2007. The livery is a revised old Midland Mainline livery with CrossCountry silver vinyls which had replaced the 'Central Trains' logo. This sequence is indeed a narrative on how often railway company franchises change and the consequent impact on railway fleets' liveries which struggle to keep up.

Opposite below: Keyham on a Summer Saturday in July 2000: Midland Mainline livery HST (unidentified) with the return working of the 07.07 Manchester Piccadilly to Newquay, 15.23 Newquay to Manchester, Saturdays only.

Bringing some unaccustomed colours to the south west, this HST reveals the original Midland Mainline teal, fawn and orange stripe livery normally seen treading the Midland main line from London St Pancras to Derby, Nottingham and Sheffield. It has just passed over Keyham viaduct, affording views over Devonport's Navy vessels in dock. The branch serving the Dockyard is seen trailing in from the lower left. Nuclear flasks form irregular traffic over this, hence the rather rusty rails.

Stoke Cutting, Devonport, Saturday, 16 July 2005: Midland Mainline HST formed of 43193 *Rio Triumph* and 43087 *Rio Invader* on hire to Virgin Trains with the 09.40 Newquay to Newcastle Saturdays Only Virgin Trains service. It had worked to Newquay earlier in the day, on the 06.51 Plymouth to Newquay after overnight stabling at Laira depot.

These 'Rio' HST sets were withdrawn from the Manchester Piccadilly to London St Pancras services in September of 2004. Here is seen one of these sets operating one of the West Country HST-operated 'Holidaymaker' trains which proved particularly popular, carrying over 10,000 passengers to and from Newquay during the peak days of the 2005 summer season. Four HSTs were hired in every weekend for a period of twelve weeks. One set, hired from GNER, fulfilled a Paignton diagram with the other three providing comfortable seating and increased capacity (as compared to that provided by the usual Voyagers) for their long-distance customers' journeys to Newquay, and enhanced with extra capacity for luggage. It was two of these three sets that were formerly used on the Midland Mainline 'Rio' services to and from Manchester. Stabling was provided at either Laira or Neville Hill. 43059 and 43060 were also in use on this date operating the 07.23 Manchester Piccadilly to Newquay, and 15.22 Newquay to Manchester Piccadilly.

This livery was launched in March 2003 and replaced that earlier version of teal and fawn seen in the previous photograph, which proved difficult to keep clean. Its darker ocean blue colour, offset with angled white and grey blocks, is perceived as one of the most effective and striking liveries of the Privatisation era.

MIDLAND PULLMAN

Approaching Britannia Crossing, Kingswear, Wednesday, 13 April 2022, Locomotive Services Ltd. 43046 in Midland Pullman livery leads the specially dedicated Pullman blue HST, with InterCity liveried 43049 at the rear, forming the 05.15 Bangor to Kingswear 'Devonian Pullman' excursion.

This view of the Dartmouth Steam Railway, adjacent to the Higher Ferry which crosses the River Dart, is close to where there was once a Halt which served workers at a local shipyard, for whom a very basic stopping service was provided. Certainly, they would have been amazed to see such an ensemble of carriages and power cars resembling the Midland Pullman which once threaded its way between London St Pancras and Manchester Central. Wearing its Nanking blue and white, it is a fine tribute to the dedicated luxury express services that were once provided in the 1960s along the Midland main line and also the Western Region line from London Paddington to Wolverhampton Low Level. There exists significant film and photographs of the original sleek trains which understandably turned onlookers' heads alongside the scenes revealing the iconic waiter service and white linen cloths for diners that underlined the concept of high quality travel. Next dream journey, the Orient Express?

NATIONAL EXPRESS

Stowmarket, Friday, 30 May 2008: Class 156 156409 in 'One' livery operating the 13.16 National Express East Anglia service from Ipswich to Cambridge past Stowmarket's GER signal box.

It may look colourful but what is it trying to say? One really can't say; it invites the potential station tannoy announcement 'The "One" train arriving at Platform one is ready for one to join it'. For a visitor to their operating region, such would be a mystery and to locals it probably just indicated a colourful splash of rainbow stripes on the cab-side and door entrance areas of the diesel multiple units. 'One' signified the combining of four previous rail operators (Anglia, Great Eastern, West Anglia, and Stansted Express) into one rail company for the whole of East Anglia. Its slogan at the time was 'All Four "one"'. Nice idea, but not quite what your average traveller would comprehend. Quite how long it took to dream this 'one' up is open to question – were there hours of deliberation in the design offices of Lawrence & Pierce or in the National Express headquarters? National Express has chosen far more sensible liveries for their electric trains which they operate in Germany – the Rhine-Münster Express and the Rhine-Wupper-Bahn contracted rail services, and three Rhine-Ruhr Express (RRX) services. Perhaps they would rather not look so whimsical within the competitive environment of Germany's complex and impressive railway network.

Ipswich, Friday, 30 May 2008: National Express East Anglia Class 90 90013 (non-branded) hauls National Express East Anglia's 12.00 Norwich to London Liverpool Street service; the coaches are in National Express East Anglia livery.

Nearly a full corporate livery displayed by this train reinforces the businesslike and uniform brand adopted in 2008 by National Express who had operated the Greater Anglia franchise from April 2004. In that franchise it combined the services previously operated by Anglia Railways, First Great Eastern and the West Anglia division of WAGN (West Anglia Great Northern). After trading as 'One' for more than three years, the company decided to rebrand as 'National Express East Anglia'. The company had previously excluded its corporate name from all its rail operations, running train companies 'one', Central Trains, and Midland Mainline among others. That changed early in 2008 when it won the franchise to replace train operator GNER; that route would be known as 'National Express East Coast'. So it was that on 11 December 2007 the first Class 90 locomotive to have been re-liveried in the revised National Express East Anglia colours was released to public view by Norwich's Crown Point depot.

NEW MEASUREMENT TRAIN (NMT)

Above: Liskeard, Friday, 10 May 2019: NMT HST passes the Down platform lower quadrant semaphore signal with the 06.06 Reading Triangle to Paignton via Penzance.

Always adding a welcome variation to the usual liveries seen in any part of the UK, these trains, essentially a development lab on rails, perform an important role with their specialist equipment which helps locate and identify faults before they become a safety issue or affect train performance. They carry the most up to date high-tech measurement systems, track scanners, and a high-resolution camera and lasers which can be used in any direction to do with track, structure gauge, OHLE (overhead line equipment) and line side infrastructure equipment positioning and clearances. They can be fitted to all sides, roofs, undersides, bogies, front, rear of all coaches and power cars forming the NMT. Lasers can be emitted from front, rear, sides, roof, bogies and underneath depending on the measurements and systems being monitored or surveyed.

Opposite above: Forder Viaduct, Friday, 9 April 2021: Colas Class 67 67023 and 67027 forming this NMT cross with the 06.08 Reading Triangle to Paignton via Penzance.

Adding further interest is this use of Colas locomotives hired in to provide the requisite traction for this monthly visitor to the Cornish main line. The attractive location features the Latchbrook Leat leading off Antony Passage, part of the Lynher river. The viaduct's graceful nine spans which stride across at 67 feet above the river estuary certainly look impressive from either side of the water, though admittedly there isn't too much here at a very low Spring tide which effectively strands those boats pictured until later. As for those on board, who wouldn't envy their boardroom view through the window?

Below: Trerulefoot, Friday, 4 June 2021: Colas owned HST power car 43299 leads the NMT set with 43290 at the rear of the 06.08 Reading Triangle to Paignton via Penzance (on its Up direction part of the diagram to Paignton).

With the western edge of Dartmoor in the background, this train which traverses the East Cornwall landscape is formed with similarly displaced HST power cars to those as seen in the photograph taken at Arley on page 92. Here is one of those HST power cars, now part of the Colas Rail fleet whilst remaining in Virgin Trains East Coast livery but now carrying the Network Rail insignia, which had previously been operating along the East Coast main line and were displaced by the IET fleet which took over LNER services out of King's Cross. The contrast in colours with the conventional yellow of the adjoining NMT carriages looks especially attractive.

Above: Churchtown Farm Bridge, near Saltash, Friday, 14 January 2022: Colas owned HST power car 43299 leads the NMT set with 43290 at the rear of the 06.08 Reading Triangle to Paignton via Penzance (on its Up direction part of the diagram to Paignton).

Just catching the edge of the shadows in the low winter sunshine, always welcome in the usual gloom of January, here is a second chance to see the same HST as appeared in the previous photograph but at the opposite end of the year. It is a reminder that an expert focus on the state of the rails and their immediate environment reflects the need for constant monitoring, for small issues such as drainage can prove highly significant in this current time of climate change, as happened with the slippage of rocks and gravel which blocked the railway line near Carmont in Scotland in August 2020 and which unfortunately derailed the Scotrail HST which encountered it with fatal consequences for two staff and one passenger. Ground- penetrating radar and CCTV surveys can all help to indicate locations where possible problems might arise and allow time to remedy the danger that might threaten the safety of passing trains.

NETWORK SOUTHEAST

Opposite above: Barking, Friday, 29 July 1994: left, Class 302 302211 with the 18.10 Barking to Shoeburyness, and right, Class 302 302202 with the 17.30 Southend Central to London Liverpool Street.

This was an occasion when London Fenchurch Street was closed for remodelling and relaying of track along the route to Barking in the summer of 1994. Hence the unusual departure and destination points of these commuter services. It is worth commenting on the extent of the overhead power lines which do not stretch over all of the London Transport Overground routes. The Class 302s provided a steady if lively ride and were a distinctive part of the railway landscape to the east of London. Slam doors remind us of a past era when safety catches avoided problems of open doors in moving trains. Now we live in an age when safety concerns require guard-operated sliding doors and it is only on preservation railways that the public need to be shown how to open and close the carriage doors.

Below: Barking, Saturday, 28 April 1990: left, a paired Derby Class 116 and BRCW Class 104 dmu (the latter out of site) arrives with the 15.45 ex-Gospel Oak, and right, Class 302 302227 paired with 308164 awaits departure with the 15.11 Shoeburyness to London Fenchurch Street.

This era of transition between BR blue and grey and Network SouthEast liveries is a reminder of the interesting variety of the intermingling of diesel and electric commuter stock within the suburbs of East London, where not all lines benefited from either third rail or overhead electrification. The blue and grey does not look tired alongside its more colourful neighbour but it does say something about the trend away from rigid BR blue that contributed to the reason why the bright and eye-catching Network SouthEast colours were welcomed, along with the much needed emphasis on running clean and punctual services as part of the Network SouthEast ethos.

Pulborough, Wednesday, 14 August 1991: Class 421 4-CIG crosses the River Arun as it departs with the 15.17 London Victoria to Bognor Regis.

  This gently flowing river passes through some fine gentle pasture and marsh land as it skirts the South Downs, and the attractive surrounding countryside is well worth exploring along the many byways. The 4-CIG electric multiple units were designed for outer-suburban routes and provided a comfortable journey with excellent viewing of the passing landscape through their windows which were matched to the seating arrangement, and not restricted by a slam door to most seating bays as with some of the contemporary commuter stock. Many more modern units have seats by pillars, even in the IETs, whereas European coaching stock usually manages to avoid this inconvenience. It becomes more of a problem if a reserved seat turns out to be alongside a pillar, though most people tend to choose to move to a different seat in the hope that it is not also reserved, much as do those who prefer to sit facing the direction of travel when allocated a seat facing the reverse direction. The IETs come equipped with green and red lights above the seating to assist indicating those seats that are available and to which station if reserved for part of the journey.

Ingatestone, Saturday, 1 July 1989. Class 309 309624 and 309621 electric multiple units operate the 18.15 Clacton to London Liverpool Street and pass the Grade II listed buildings which date from 1846.

These 'Clacton Express' units could turn an impressive speed on the Anglian main line, being capable of 100mph, and and they proved popular for their high level of comfort thanks to their second and first class compartments – a feature usually reserved for InterCity hauled stock. These trains would divide at Thorpe-le-Soken, with one of the four-car units used on the Walton section, and the remaining six cars continuing to Clacton.

After 1985, when electrification spread north from Colchester to Ipswich, and later to Harwich, these units extended their field of use on fast trains to Ipswich and Harwich. Their smart, distinctive appearance impressed the lineside photographers throughout their careers, with the last unit withdrawn in January 1994.

Regional Railways North West then acquired seven redundant units for use on suburban passenger services from Manchester Piccadilly to Crewe and Stoke-on-Trent, with one daily diagram as far as Birmingham. This seems to have been a low-key appearance rather than a swan song for the Class.

Seaton Junction, Saturday, 22 July 1989: Class 50 50050 *Fearless* passes with the 17.15 London Waterloo to Exeter St Davids.

This station may have closed in March 1966, but it has retained its canopies and station buildings, primarily thanks to private ownership. Whether anybody at the time of its closure would have envisaged the location becoming part of the widely-embracing Network SouthEast empire, whose tentacles reached as far west as Exeter, is highly unlikely. The term 'SouthEast' seems somewhat tenuous in its links to this East Devon location – but because the line served London Waterloo, it was incorporated into the maze that formed the Network SouthEast map. If there was to be a corporate colour for trains entering the London Waterloo hub of London commuter land, then that logically applied to trains running on all routes serving Waterloo, hence Honiton, Pinhoe and Exeter Central were included, with haulage by Network SouthEast livery Class 50s. After all, they had been part of the London and South Western Railway and therefore they had previous links with that company's network of routes. As for Network SouthEast travel promotion days, for a ten pound note it was possible to visit anywhere in the rest of the Network SouthEast territory – Clacton, Canterbury or Cambridge all became possible destinations for the determined visitor from the South West, even if it meant a break-of-dawn initial car journey for those joining from points west of Exeter.

Royal Albert Bridge, Saturday, 23 November 1991: Class 50 50033 *Glorious* heads Pathfinder Tours' 'The Valiant Thunderer' en route from Manchester Piccadilly to Newquay.

For photographers and passengers, excursions featuring locomotives in distinct regional liveries which are visiting out-of-region locations will always be an acceptable exception to the rule of a livery keeping strictly within the geographical area of its regional identity, such as Network SouthEast, and this location well to the west of Laira depot, which serviced the Class 50 fleet, is clearly justified for one such case – and no doubt there will be enthusiasts on board purely for the exhilarating ride that the Class 50 would offer to them. Thus 'Network SouthEast' colours will embrace the Cornish landscape once this train crosses over the iconic bridge, although it may be that a passport is requisite for participants to enter the Royal Duchy at Saltash. Indeed, in their heyday, Class 50s in this livery would regularly reach Newquay on summer Saturdays in 1987, the last year of locomotive haulage on the Newquay branch.

Waterside, Dartmouth Steam Railway, Saturday, 23 May 1998: Class 50 50002 *Superb* in Network SouthEast livery with a late afternoon train from Paignton to Kingswear.

Torbay always looks splendid in the sunshine, whichever season, and the Class 50 in this livery looks very much at home. I sometimes wonder about whether those who stay in the chalets in the Holiday Park realise what a treat they are in for with so many interesting trains passing close by, each making an immense noise when ascending the steep gradient of 1 in 71. I suspect that at least some of these ladies and gentlemen have a latent interest in trains just waiting to be revived when here on holiday.

East Croydon, Saturday, 30 May 1992: Class 33/1 33114 *Ashford 150* in Network SouthEast livery hauls restored 4TCs with a London Bridge to Ashford 'Ashford 150' commemorative train after its naming earlier that same morning.

This was a lucky chance for a photograph of such a special train, as I was merely changing trains when it passed by. Until the electrification of the Bournemouth to Weymouth route in 1988 these Class 33/1s saw daily use on Bournemouth to Weymouth trains, which originated at London Waterloo as 12-carriage formations powered by 4REP (Restaurant Electro-Pneumatic brake) electric multiple units on the rear with two leading units of un-powered 4TCs (Trailer Control) . At Bournemouth, the Class 33/1 attached to the two sets of 4TCs and hauled the revised train formation westwards to Weymouth. I recall these making a splendid noise ascending Bincombe bank with London-bound services in the late 1980s, as well as pairs of Class 33s substituting for Class 50s on the Exeter to London Waterloo services in October 1988.

NORTHERN RAIL

Ravenglass, Thursday, 13 August 2009: Northern Rail Class 156 in Northern livery departs with the 13.31 Barrow-in-Furness to Carlisle service. The train is crossing the viaduct across the River Mite.

   This Cumbrian Coast line is sometimes overlooked in terms of dramatic landscape, with its coastal and Lake District mountain scenery, spectacular viaducts and views over the Solway Firth towards Scotland at its northern end, along with Sellafield's controversial presence, all offering vistas of interest and intrigue. The lengthy journey is well worthwhile and a circular route taken by returning via the West Coast main line can make for an absorbing itinerary.

St Bees, Thursday, 15 April 2010: Northern Class 156 156438 arrives with the 15.12 Carlisle to Preston.
 The railway through St Bees was opened on 1 June 1849 and the station opened in July 1849. The present imposing red sandstone station building was built in 1860. The railway attracted the professional classes commuting to Whitehaven, and this led to the building of many of the larger houses in St Bees, which is a small Cumbrian coast town with plenty of character. The line has just passed through a valley which provided excellent acoustics for northward departing Class 37/4s when these locomotives stood in for a shortage of dmus with rakes of hauled carriages during following years – with their dedicated enthusiast clientele on board.

Morchard Road, Saturday, 9 April 2011: First Great Western Class 142 142067 in Northern livery arrives with the 13.53 Exmouth/14.27 Exeter St Davids to Barnstaple.

Here is a lost interloper from the North West traipsing the rural depths of Devon's branch line railways – quite a change of scenery from the Mancunian routes that it had previously operated on, although it had been based at Exeter since autumn 2008. It escaped any possibility of being preserved, unlike some of its kin, as it was scrapped in January 2020, having served for much longer than its builders probably intended. They were entitled 'Nodding Donkeys' because of the rocking motion that these trains endured when rolling on the rails – maybe the intention was to avoid too many day trip passengers travelling to Blackpool from feeling they really needed an additional ride on the funfair's Big Dipper!

Manston, Saturday, 29 May 2021: Class 331/1 'Civity' four-car outer suburban electric multiple unit in New Northern livery passes with the 11.33 Leeds to Ilkley

At last, for the UK market, we are able to enjoy a train designed for passengers who actually wish to view the pleasant passing Yorkshire Dales springtime countryside through landscape windows with comfortable tables and seating. It has taken a Spanish train builder to do this (CAF). Likewise, similar trains have been supplied recently to passengers travelling direct from Liverpool to Blackpool, also enjoying a new link without having to change at Preston. Certainly, the travel experience of passengers on board has been improved, although the displaced Class 333s, an equally successful train built by CAF between 2000 and 2003, still see service intermingled with these units at the time of writing.

PARCELS

Hemerdon Bank, Saturday, 24 September 1983: Class 45 45048 *The Royal Marines* climbs at full thrust with a mid- afternoon parcels train.

It may be short, but at least it is a parcels service on a Saturday, both of which would be a dream for UK railway photographers today. Rather like the way in which buses reflect their owning company liveries, and these become an established part of the colours on parade in their operating area, so this train simply wears its 'standard' BR Parcels blue and grey – it was taken for granted at this time that a reliable mail and parcels service was to be provided without the perceived need to apply a high profile dedicated livery or brand. Admittedly, in the current decade, with the exception of Switzerland, no such dedicated and specialised trains feature in the railway traffic of Europe. French Railways (SNCF) operated on behalf of the French post office, *La Poste*, a fleet of five half TGV sets carrying post between Marseille and Paris until June 2015, and then switched the movement of post by rail from TGVs to standardised swap-bodies. The concept was interesting as it used the dedicated high speed lines to deliver post from city centre to city centre, with a journey time of around three hours. Long distances between cities across France are less favoured to movement of parcels by road, and one assumes such is now conveyed by aircraft. At least they gave it a try – the exact opposite to the British post office which during 2003 decided to suspend *all* transportation of mail by rail, claiming it was uneconomic. Interestingly, bulk transfer services along the West Coast Main Line between its mail terminals at London (Willesden), Warrington and Glasgow (Shieldmuir) were later reintroduced using a small fleet of adapted Class 325 electric multiple units.

Plymouth Laira Depot, Monday, 23 December 1996 : left, a newly liveried Great Western Trains Swallow livery carriage-set; centre, Propelling Control Vehicle (PCV) four-car set in Rail Express livery, recently introduced to service in its new role after conversion from Class 307 DVTs; right, InterCity liveried HST power cars back-to-back.

The PCV conversion of the displaced Class 307 DVTs (which had previously operated on commuter services along the Great Eastern and London, Tilbury and Southend lines) proved useful in assisting with the need to reverse mail trains into the Royal Mail Distribution Centres. The driving trailers were used to propel their trains into or out of these termini, thus operated in push-pull mode with a locomotive. Such meant there was no need, on arrival, to run around the locomotive to the other end of the train for later haulage onto the railway network, an otherwise time-consuming process. Windows and slam-doors were replaced by roller-shutter doors, and a modernised cab – all features clearly shown on the vehicle in this photograph.

Above: Cockwood Harbour, Tuesday, 20 July 1993: front, Class 47/7 47712 *Lady Diana Spencer* in parcels red livery and 'second' Class 47/7 47581 in Rail Express Systems livery with the 16.45 Plymouth to York parcels train. 47581 was renumbered 47763 by the following January.

Here is an interesting opportunity to compare the earlier BR red and grey Parcels livery and the later Rail Express Systems livery with horizontal blue bands and graphite grey applied to the top third of the locomotive. Incorporating Post Office colours of Royal Mail red, the parcels carrying operations of British Rail became Rail Express Systems in 1991, and the locomotives and coaching stock received this high profile livery as part of the recognised need to rebrand this specialised sector. Here, business needs dictated the livery which was selected in a very eye-catching manner. Two of the fleet of carriages are so branded as seen immediately behind the locomotives in this train consist.

Opposite below: Salford Crescent, Thursday, 31 May 1990: left, Class 31 31238 wearing Trainload Freight Petroleum Roundel livery leads Class 31 31203 with a northbound tanker train, probably destined for Teeside; right, Derby Class 114 Parcels dmu convert 55930 (ex-53010) and 54900 (ex-55933/56034) is seen bound for Manchester Victoria carrying Royal Mail letters.

The diagonal yellow stripes mark the location of the roller shutter doors which were a necessary modification of this previously passenger unit and were fitted at the locations of the two passenger doors, this work being undertaken at Ilford. They merge well with the immaculate predominant Post Office red and the yellow lines along the solebar of this dmu. These converted vehicles saw use for the Parcels Sector between October 1986 and October 1990.

Below: Redhill, Tuesday, 25 July 1995: Class 47/7 locos 47710 *Lady Godiva* in Waterman Railways black livery and 47761 in Rail Express Systems livery, stabled at the south end of the station.

Both locomotives seen here are dedicated to the Parcels sector, with the black livery Class 47 47710 having transferred to this sector in June 1993. It had previously been named *Sir Walter Scott* in September 1979 and acquired its Waterman 'Heritage Class' style plates, which were fitted at mid-height on the bodyside, on 28 June 1994. It may be somewhat intriguing that a locomotive should be named after an English Lady who had ridden through Coventry naked, to persuade her husband to reduce his heavy taxes. In fact, this nameplate featured in a series of names adopted by Waterman Railways as part of a theme of heroes and heroines of real life and fiction. The locomotive was bestowed with the name at Coventry station.

PULLMAN

Plymouth, Friday, 9 July 2021: rear, in Pullman livery, West Coast Railway Class 57/6 57601 *Windsor Castle* with West Coast Railway Class 57/3 57314 (and with Class 47/4 47802 heading the train) tail at the rear of the delayed 'Northern Belle Diner' return excursion to Bristol Temple Meads from Plymouth (its intended destination of Par was aborted owing to problems with the Class 57/3).

The splendid umber and cream borne by the locomotive and coaching stock is very impressive, and diners on board will hopefully appreciate this embellishment carried by the Mk.2 ex-InterCity First class carriages, each with its interior carefully restored to a high standard providing their very comfortable seating whilst they munch their way through some very tasty cuisine. If after arriving at the train's destination they need to then change to a Great Western Railway IET they may be in for a shock, as the seating provided on those trains has been compared unfavourably to ironing boards.

REGIONAL RAILWAYS

Terras Crossing, Tuesday, 3 August 1993: Gloucester RCW Class 122 dmus front, 55012 in Regional Railways livery and rear, 55003 in BR blue and white with the 16.25 Looe to Liskeard.

A well loaded late afternoon train carries its happy day trippers back home after a day at the beach and no doubt well filled with ice creams and Cornish pasties – clearly the strengthened formation is well justified. The tide is low and there is no risk of a high tide for quite some time – Spring tides can render the road just beyond the crossing below several inches of salt water. The train must stop and give a shrill hoot before proceeding – the junction behind the photographer effectively means car drivers turning off the main road get very little advance warning of an approaching train, with their vision to the right blocked by vegetation.

RAIL OPERATIONS GROUP (ROG)

Gatcombe, near Purton, Tuesday, 5 October 2021: Class 57 57312 passes with the late-running 08.43 Crewe South Yard to Newport Docks towing Class 365s, withdrawn by Great Northern from service in May 2021, for scrap.

This train is passing along the River Severn, which is tidal at this point, and not far from the location of the twenty-one span Severn (railway) Bridge at Sharpness, on the other side of the water, that crossed over to nearby Lydney and which was fatefully damaged beyond repair by a tanker vessel which destroyed a pier and two spans of the bridge in October 1960. ROG provides the sort of service featured in this photograph and promotes itself as supplying specialist services relating to rolling stock movements. It has developed an eye-catching futuristic blue livery which certainly stands out when compared to the colours worn by the recently withdrawn unit.

SCOTRAIL

Edinburgh Waverley, Thursday, 14 April 2011: First ScotRail Class 170/4 170473 in Strathclyde PTE livery departs with the 15.31 to Dunblane.

The wires are there but the train must be formed of a diesel multiple unit as completion of electrification of the line between Polmont Junction through Stirling and to Dunblane would only come over seven years later. The height of the surrounding building (the Scottish National Gallery), above the Mound Tunnel, reminds us that Edinburgh Waverley sits in a deep cutting – which remarkably divides the city – and must be accessed and exited by a series of escalators, the exit ramp by road being inaccessible to passengers. Prior to these escalators, the good citizens of Edinburgh could take pride in keeping super fit by having to ascend them by leg-power. The old adage 'Let the Train take the Strain' for them would have taken on a rather different perspective.

Dalmeny, Friday, 4 September 2020: ScotRail Class 170/4 170412 exits the Forth bridge with the 11.21 Cowdenbeath to Edinburgh Waverley.

Such an iconic structure entirely deserves the many plaudits which it has received since its construction, and the journey crossing over the bridge offers unrivalled views of the Firth of Forth over which it towers, providing a majestic tribute to Victorian railway engineering. Artists, photographers, authors and engineers provide their own style of reverent applause to its attributes through their images and creations to capture its splendour, be it from down at the coastline below the bridge or here on a level with its entrance archway beckoning those journeying on trains entering to contemplate the intricacies of the metallic gargantuan structure bedecked in a striking red hue. It cannot fail to impress with its fusion of girders, interlacing diagonal iron joints and tubes that knit together the three double-cantilever towers, crossing the sometimes turbulent tidal currents below at a height of 150 feet (46 meters) above high water. It is also a memorial to the 73 men who died while working in the construction of the bridge. Their legacy is indeed one of the pinnacles of worldwide engineering.

Opposite above: Glasgow Central, Monday, 18 April 2011: First ScotRail Class 380 Desiro electric multiple units: left: 380105, and right, 380003 forming the 11.50 to Wemyss Bay.

These electric units were introduced to Scotland's railways in December 2010, when on 8 December 380111 worked the 1Z33 16.26 Paisley Gilmour Street to Ayr additional service, the first Class 380 in public service. Their initial area of operation was in Ayrshire and Inverclyde, but they have since spread their wings to serve on routes across the Scottish Lowlands including Glasgow Central to Edinburgh via Carstairs. The newly applied Saltire Blue livery proves eye-catching.

When Central station was expanded between 1899 and 1905, the original roof was kept, but the new section had arched ironwork rather than the traditional horizontal ironwork. The arched supports can here be seen clearly, springing from the pillars on either side of the middle canopy. The extension involved not only these dramatic canopies but also decorative stonework which has clearly had a recent thorough clean. There are apparently 48,000 panes of glass across the station, which must take some determined effort to keep clean.

Below: Stonehaven, Friday, 15 April 2011: First ScotRail Turbostar Class 170/4 170421 arrives with the 13.06 Aberdeen to Edinburgh, 13.22 from Stonehaven.

Here is a fine top-lit timber canopy, cantilevered over the platform on cast columns with large scrolled Caledonian Railway ironwork brackets. Out of sight is the station building, dating from 1849 and in Italianate style. The station is about a mile from the beach and harbour, as it is set towards the back of the town – dictated by the need for the line to keep height along the contours of the surrounding rolling countryside. At this date, Class 170 diesel multiple units could be seen operating many non-electrified routes in Scotland, with the exception of the West Highland lines; however as a result of the electrification of the Edinburgh to Glasgow Queen Street line in 2018 and the conversion of ScotRail Express services to Aberdeen and Inverness to HSTs in 2018-20, a substantial number of the Class have since been displaced from ScotRail.

Clachnaharry, Friday, 17 September 2021: ScotRail Class 158 passes over the swingbridge across the entrance to the Caledonian Canal with the 10.41 Inverness to Wick.

This serene setting with the Beauly Firth in the background is photographed from the lock gates at the north end of Muirtown Basin, situated on the mouth of the Caledonian Canal where it joins the Beauly Firth. From here the canal can be navigated as far as Corpach, near Fort William and close to the station situated next to the lock gates there.

The swing bridge crosses the canal at an angle of 65 degrees and is electrically controlled from the signal box seen here at the west end of the bridge. The 2-storey, weather-boarded signal box, which is Category B Listed, was built for the Highland Railway in 1890. Noteworthy is the timber outside stairs to the raised doorway in the projecting, half-gabled porch. The signal box contains a small mechanical lever frame with four levers labelled 'Up', 'Down' and 'Bridge Locks'. Many local dog-walkers, cyclists and inquisitive visitors to the footpath on the far side of the crossing seem to entirely disregard the notice which indicates that it is a 'private level crossing for authorised users only' and I needed only to catch the eye of the friendly signalman to cross over, once the train had passed by.

Stirling, Friday, 10 September 2021: ScotRail HST, with power car 43031 at the rear, calls with the 13.50 Aberdeen to Glasgow Queen Street.

These ScotRail HSTs, refurbished for Abellio, form a fleet of seventeen five-car and nine four-car sets to link seven Scottish cities and branded *Inter7City*, providing an InterCity quality of service not provided by Class 170s. The overhauled and modified Great Western HST power cars and trailers were cascaded from their traditional West Country territory and have taken over many diagrams previously allocated to ScotRail Class 170 Turbostar dmus which are now reallocated to different operators while the HSTs extend their wings. Slateford has been used for their storage and cold stabling to relieve pressure on the ever crowded Haymarket depot. Not all has gone smoothly, for these are 40-year-old trains and extensive corrosion and other ageing issues after storage needed attention. Some trailer sets were placed into service with little remedial attention – initially, even the seating was that previously used by GWR. Some of the refurbished sets demonstrated evidence of poor quality workmanship but gradually quality of the refurbishments and performance of the 'Classic' sets improved with experience, and their reliability has much improved. Some of the early teething problems related to the harsher Scottish winter weather – somewhat colder than they were used to. In time, all may be eventually extended to 5 car sets.

SILVERLINK

Woburn Sands, Friday, 4 June 1999: front, Class 121 Pressed Steel dmu 55027 in Silverlink Trains livery, and 'rear' Class 121 Pressed Steel dmu 55031 in Network SouthEast livery operating the 16.20 Bedford to Bletchley.

Here is a scene recalling earlier eras of railway architecture and motive power. The LNWR signal box, semaphore signals and station buildings create an impression more from the 1960s than at the turn of the millennium.

Woburn Sands station opened in November 1846; its station building conveys a Flemish influence seen in its high pitched gables with pierced decorative bargeboards. At platform level there was a booking office, booking hall, ladies' waiting room and general waiting room. The Victorian signal box was dismantled in August 2004. Named the Marston Vale line, this sixteen miles long rural branch line remains characterful, passing agricultural land and intermittent sites of previous brickworks (there were several along the route including Eastwood's at Woburn Sands). Historically it formed a link in the chain from Oxford to Cambridge, but in 1967 the line was curtailed to its current form with trains withdrawn from Bletchley to Oxford and from Bedford to Cambridge. It has since been modernised and has an active Community Rail Partnership. If plans come to fruition, there will be two trains per hour along the route, operating between Bletchley and Cambridge. A further two trains will run the full length of the line, between Oxford and Cambridge.

Three Vivarail two-car Class 230 D Train diesel electric multiple units (DEMUs) entered traffic on the Bedford-Bletchley line from April 23, 2019, replacing Class 150 Sprinter diesel units.

Exeter St Davids, Saturday, 9 April 2011: First Great Western Class 150 150130 in Silverlink livery, operating the 14.43 Barnstaple to Exmouth.

Displaced from its previous areas of service along the Marston Vale Bedford to Bletchley line (it actually carried a nameplate *Bedford-Bletchley 150*) and the Gospel Oak-Barking line, this train with its colourful livery could be seen treading paths around South Devon for a time, before finally receiving First Great Western blue. One wonders how many of its passengers in the South West actually appreciated this 'link' with Silverlink or had ever travelled along those lines where it once had been such a familiar sight.

SOMERSET AND DORSET JOINT RAILWAY

Bishops Lydeard, West Somerset Railway, Saturday, 21 March 2009: Class 7F 2-8-0 88 returns in a light engine movement to collect its next train. The 7Fs in the early days of the S&DJR are remembered for their distinctive Prussian Blue livery with gold lettering.

Built in 1925, this Fowler design locomotive for the Somerset and Dorset Joint Railway (S&DJR) is one of two of this Class which survived through to preservation and looks splendid in its restored S&DJR livery. It was preserved on loan to the West Somerset Railway (WSR) by the Somerset and Dorset Railway Trust, which until recently has been based at Washford, as this site with its former goods yard enabled the trust to develop and promote itself along with its museum, including restoration of a number of former S&DJR goods wagons and coaches, as well as *Kilmersdon* – a Peckett 0-4-0ST locomotive. 88 has featured in many of the line's steam galas over the last two decades, having been associated with the WSR since its restoration to service in September 1987, but has now moved on to pastures new at the Mid Hants Railway. This followed some unfortunate political wrangling involving the role of the Trust and the WSR PLC's decision to terminate the S&D Trust's lease of the Washford site.

Roebuck Farm, West Somerset Railway, Saturday, 24 March 2007: Class 7F 2-8-0 88 passing with the 14.25 Bishops Lydeard to Minehead.

Indeed, much enjoyed by local and visiting steam enthusiasts for photography and travel behind this splendid locomotive – which was such a graceful and genuine part of the West Somerset scene – is 88's regretted departure from the West Somerset Railway, and the accompanying closure of the Washford site referred to above. It appears evident that there had been a significant breakdown in communication between the WSR PLC and the S & D Trust to the extent that it has been reported extensively in railway media albeit with neither side emerging positively and with apparently justified criticism of both parties' attitudes and responses. It is hoped, at the time of writing, that discussions for the S&D Trust to remain at Washford on a ten year lease as part of a new agreement may offer a positive and constructive way forward.

Here in happier days is seen this locomotive working on the line that was its home for so long – a rural Somerset landscape and an air of tranquillity and ease away from the busyness of the modern world which seems here so far away.

SOUTHERN

Hastings, Friday, 3 September 2021: Southern TurboStar Class 171/4 171401 arrives with a mid-morning service from Brighton and Eastbourne to Ashford.

The ornate road bridge and Hastings tunnel entrance greet west-bound trains, and remind us of the hilly terrain at the back of Hastings. The third rail does not extend along the route to Rye and Ashford, and DEMUs powered by English Electric engines once 'thumped' (an enthusiast's term recalling the engine's sound) or throbbed their way eastwards across Winchelsea and Romney Marshes, the latter with its characteristic churches occupying tufts of raised ground, amidst fields of grazing sheep munching abundant grass, like ships at sea.

This Class 171/4 had been previously treading the rails of Scotland, as part of the ScotRail Class 170 fleet, and has been rebuilt and reformed into a four-car unit.

Opposite below: Billingshurst, Saturday, 26 June 2021: Southern ElectroStar Class 377/1 377 106 passes with the 10.13 Southampton to London Victoria

The Retro style architecture of the pub facade is a reminder that it was built at the same time as the railway, and its purpose was evidently to provide refreshments and also accommodation. The red and cream colour scheme brushes with the Southern green of the ornate railway footbridge, which the modern express electric unit will shortly pass below at some speed, no doubt offering this scene as a glimpse into the past for travellers heading for London. The previous level crossing gates would have required the (now closed) local signal box to operate, with traffic observed and the gates closed with plenty of time to allow the approaching train to pass, thus avoiding problems with automatic barriers which may close on queuing traffic and which necessitates the yellow grid box, as seen here, about which the Highway Code's instruction 'You MUST NOT enter the box until your exit road or lane is clear' is especially requisite when painted on road crossings on the main line railway.

SOUTHERN RAILWAY (SR)

Below: Horsted Keynes, Bluebell Railway, Sunday, 24 October 2010: Southern Railway Class U 2-6-0 1638 departs with a late afternoon Pullman Dining Train to Sheffield Park.

The late afternoon sun glints off the smart livery of both 1638 and its fine set of historic carriages, so forming a timepiece in which they are perfectly matched to the hues of the autumnal trees. Such a scene could well have embellished the North Downs line along which this engine found itself working when, following the electrification of the Brighton line in 1933, it was reallocated to Guildford.

Even the 1938-built London Midland & Scottish Railway Stove R 6-wheel gangwayed Guard's Brake coach behind the locomotive, the design of which was of an entirely different nature altogether from its Southern compatriots, blends in to the scene alongside its Pullman cousin *Fingall*. This was built by the Birmingham Railway Carriage and Wagon Co. for the Yorkshire Pullman and later saw use on the Southern Region, including the Bournemouth Belle. It is now to be seen regularly running in the Bluebell Railway's Golden Arrow Pullman Dining Train. What a wonderful experience for diners on board and a real feast for the lineside photographers.

Above: Horsted Keynes, Bluebell Railway, Sunday, 24 October 2010: Southern Railway Class E4 0-6-2T 473 *Birch Grove* departs with the 12.43 service from Horsted Keynes to Sheffield Park. Judging by how well the natural autumnal greens and yellows displayed by the surrounding trees complement this passing train, the Southern Railway livery can be considered a perfect partner to the surroundings through which the company's locomotives and rolling stock passed, once away from the urban sprawl and threading their way through the rolling countryside of Kent, Surrey and Sussex. Many modern liveries look sleek but often somewhat metallic – rather like the current 'Southern' livery. In an environmentally conscious age, maybe the quest for seeking nature and a more natural lifestyle will extend to train liveries.

SOUTH EASTERN AND CHATHAM RAILWAY

Opposite above: Horsted Keynes, Bluebell Railway, Sunday, 24 October 2010: Wainwright design locomotives, front, SECR Class P 0-6-0T 31178 and second, SECR Class C 0-6-0 31592 depart with the 11.33 service from Horsted Keynes to Sheffield Park.

This pair of locomotives excel with their elegant design features complemented by immaculate SECR paintwork here highlighted by the morning sunlight. The 'full Wainwright' lined green livery for SECR locomotives, beautifully finished with complex lining and burnished brass dome covers, was one of the most elaborate and decorative to be seen in the UK.

Immediately behind them is the similarly exuberant GNR Directors' Saloon 706E, LNER 43909. This magnificent clerestory saloon was constructed in 1897 and used by the GNR/LNER directors, then British Railways Eastern Region General Manager until 1969. Superbly restored to its GNR/LNER appearance, it has always remained available for special-traffic use since first arriving at the Bluebell in October 1971.

SOUTHEASTERN

Below: Wadhurst, Friday, 3 September 2021: Class 375/7 'ElectroStar' 375707 arrives with the 10.15 Charing Cross to Hastings service.

There is certainly a blue theme here – apart from the Southeastern blue electric multiple unit, we see a blue and white bridge, blue seats, blue bands on the station light poles, and blue metallic covers in the 'six foot'. Along with the canopy over the Up platform waiting room, there is certainly some railway atmosphere at the location, all for the benefit of the single passenger awaiting his train. The modern and sleek appearance of these electric units is echoed by their comfortable interiors and spacious leg room, tables and landscape windows – a modern design train which actually has the traveller in mind rather than the economies of fitting in as many seats as possible, some alongside pillars rather than windows, as has been the evident aim of previous generations of suburban trains.

SOUTH WEST TRAINS AND SOUTH WESTERN RAILWAY

Eastleigh, Saturday, 16 October 1999: Class 442 'Wessex Express' 2423 in South West Trains livery passes with the 11.30 London Waterloo to Weymouth.

The "Wessex Express" five-car Class 442s were popular with enthusiasts for their attractive curvaceous cabs, and operated services on the London to Dorset Coast route from the late 1980's until their replacement by Class 444s from 2007. They were then stored at Eastleigh with a view to further use, but the post-pandemic downturn in travel has meant that their planned refurbishment was cancelled and they were subsequently permanently withdrawn in 2021. Part of the Stagecoach empire, South West Trains operated over a much larger area than was always credited, with its tentacles not only serving South West London, but also extending to West Dorset (Weymouth and Dorchester) and stations well to the west within Somerset and Devon, reaching as far as Honiton and Exeter St Davids – thus inheriting the famed route of the Atlantic Coast Express. With reference to the latter, the very short-sighted singling in 1967 of long sections of the route west of Salisbury by British Railways has left a legacy of problems when trains run late (either way) and consequently cause further delay to trains coming in the opposite direction, which are required to await the opportunity to pass and continue their journey. Fortunately, several extensive loops have more recently been installed at strategic locations, such as at Axminster, which has done much to mitigate this avoidable disadvantage.

Near Ely, by the River Great Ouse, Wednesday, 28 May 2008: South West Trains two-car Class 158/8 operated by East Midlands Trains passes with the 11.36 service from Peterborough to Norwich.

This is either refurbished (converted from previous Trans-Pennine Express operations) Class 158/8 884, 886 or 887, based at Salisbury, whilst on loan and subleased to East Midlands Trains (EMT), a sister Stagecoach franchise, after accident damage to an EMT Class 158/8 in late January 2008 and after a previous two South West Trains Class 158/8s were placed on hire since November 2007. Thus this visitor provides the unusual sight of a South West Trains unit running 'under the wires'.

Axminster, Tuesday, 15 June 2021: South Western Railway Class 159/1 159101 departs with the 11.25 Exeter St Davids to London Waterloo.

    It may be in the previous operator's livery, in Stagecoach colours, but this diesel unit now belongs to a jointly-operated franchise, South Western Railway, owned by FirstGroup and MTR Corporation. The train is departing the Down platform, used when there is no requirement to pass another service, but at least the loop provides for such a need. From a low point during the 1970s and 1980s, when trains ran around once every two hours each way, there is a much-improved hourly service west of Yeovil. During the decades covered by this book, the route was of interest to enthusiasts seeking lengthy runs behind locomotives as it was ruled by Class 50s and then by Class 47/7s, with the occasional pairing of Class 33s to add flavour. The rolling hills west of Salisbury provided a chance to hear the engines working hard, and at speed on the South West 'fast' line between Basingstoke and London Waterloo.

STRATHCLYDE PTE

Glasgow Central, Thursday, 10 August 1995: left, Class 303 303010 in Strathclyde PTE livery departs with an early evening rush hour service, while on the right simultaneously a Class 86/4 in Rail Express Systems livery departs with a southbound Travelling Post Office service.

The mid-nineties' rail scene was certainly colourful, whichever region of the UK you lived in, and Glasgow reflects the interesting variety that was an everyday occurrence. Perhaps the local train will take a route incorporating part of the Cathcart Circle – providing an interesting challenge for those rail enthusiasts who wish to travel over all available lines on which passenger trains travel in Great Britain. To ensure all parts of the line are travelled over in both directions means you need a very good sense of direction accompanied by a compass and a comprehensive local train timetable.

101 694

Opposite above: Glasgow Central, Friday, 11 August 1995: right, Class 303 303009 in Strathclyde PTE livery with the 14.35 to Newton via Longside and left, Class 101 Metro-Cammell DMU 51188/53268 in Strathclyde PTE livery with the 14.38 to Paisley Canal.

The fine lighting permitted by the station's expansive grand glass roof highlights the cross girders and arches as well as the local inhabitants awaiting their next suburban journeys, with both types of train surviving now only within preservation. The Class 303s were especially well regarded in terms of their aesthetic appearance, and were known as the 'Glasgow Blue Train' when placed in service on the North Clyde routes in November 1960 wearing their original livery of 'Caledonian blue' with yellow and black lining, and grey roofs.

Opposite below: Stirling, Friday, 2 June 2000: viewed from the south end of the station, Class 156 156495 in Strathclyde PTE Carmine and Cream livery awaits departure with the 10.41 Dunblane to Glasgow Queen Street.

The Category A Listed station building and the glazed awnings covering the platforms with their decorative cast-iron columns continue to impress visitors to this gem of station architecture. Fortunately, electrification undertaken here since this image was taken has been relatively unintrusive. The lengthy platforms seem to swallow up the small two-car diesel unit, for the station harks back to the days of long locomotive hauled trains heading towards the Highlands.

TRANSPORT FOR WALES

Below: Purton, Tuesday, 5 October 2021: Class 170 TurboStar 170271, previously operated by Greater Anglia whose livery it still carries, passes with the 13.59 Gloucester to Cardiff and Maesteg.

Here is a livery which is effectively incorrect for a unit operated by Transport for Wales, for it has yet to be repainted – but at this distance it looks smart enough and stands out against its picturesque background of the River Severn estuary and the pleasant Gloucestershire countryside. There's the rub – for if the livery is not so crucial to the presentation of the train, then why spend vast amounts of money developing projects to design a distinctive livery for a train which, taken at a distance, could be any one of the various conglomerate modern liveries in the UK? If you seek a highly visible distinctive livery, try that displayed by TransPennine Express or look to the nearby continent, especially the Italian Railways' ETR.400 Frecciarossa High Speed trains.

TRANSPENNINE EXPRESS

Above: Kirkham Abbey, Sunday, 26 September 2021: A Class 68 in TransPennine livery passes the station house with a mid-morning Scarborough-bound train, in push-mode.

Now here is a livery which catches the eye both from close up and from a distance – you can't fail to notice it. With the impressive Class 68 locomotives in charge of several Manchester to Scarborough rosters at the time of this image, their dynamic livery certainly conveys a sense of robust purpose and power, although use on that route faced several problems in 2021 including complaints by the Scarborough residents living near the railway who expressed annoyance at the noise and light at night coming from the Seamer depot. The surrounding valley here definitely resounded to the noise of the departing train, which continued to be heard well in to the far distance.

Opposite above: Kirkham Abbey, Sunday, 26 September 2021: A pair of Class 185 diesel units, with 185141 leading, heads for York with the 11.21 from Scarborough.

The high volume of trains departing Scarborough on a late summer Sunday morning suggests that there are vast numbers of people returning home after a night out at the resort, and they are well catered for. The adjacent characterful signal box just out of sight to the left was certainly kept busy operating the crossing gates for such a procession. No doubt some of the passengers on board may be less interested in the angular designed livery to the rear of the cab and more interested in seeking a cure for a hangover.

Below: Kirkham Abbey, Sunday, 26 September 2021: A Class 68 '68023', in TransPennine livery passes near the Abbey ruins with the 10.34 Scarborough to York service, in push-mode.

The trend for locomotive-hauled trains both in the UK and Western Europe to be replaced by diesel or electric units is here challenged by the interesting policy of TransPennine to reintroduce this type of traction. The reduced timetable caused by the Covid pandemic combined with the winter timetable of 2022 saw just four locomotives working diagrams mainly to and from York and Scarborough with only a very few extending to Manchester or Liverpool at the time of writing. The accompanying Mark 5A coaches reflect the vivid livery applied to the Class 68. Passengers on board can enjoy the North Yorkshire countryside whilst listening to the throb of the Class 68; I recall the halcyon days of Class 40s whistling their way along the same route on regular Liverpool Lime Street to Scarborough two-hourly services.

Near Ely, Wednesday, 28 May 2008: An East Midlands Trains Class 158, which is an ex-TransPennine Express unit in revised TransPennine Express livery (with the blue lower-bodyside branding having been removed and Central vinyls applied), is seen passing Ely Cathedral with the 11.57 Norwich to Peterborough/Liverpool Lime Street service. It was one of four Class 158 units which were also operated by Central Trains on transfer from TransPennine Express.

This is a particularly striking example of how when some units are transferred between operators, the livery is not immediately replaced, understandably, but the original livery becomes diluted with various insignia to remind viewers that it now belongs to a different company than indicated by the main livery. Such complexities usually make the railway press and prove of interest if not confusion to photographers visiting the area.

TRANSRAIL FREIGHT

Forder viaduct, Friday, 23 July 1999: Class 37s, the front one in Transrail livery and the second in Civil Engineers livery, with an early evening east-bound china clay train for Stoke.

The Transrail livery of two-tone grey with Transrail logos, a blue and red 'T', could well be argued not to be a genuine livery. Transrail, along with Loadhaul and Mainline Freight, was formed in 1994, when British Rail decided to concentrate its freight operations in three 'shadow freight' companies. To achieve this, BR divided the country into three regions, with Transrail operating in the west. Whilst Loadhaul and Mainline bestowed new livery designs, Transrail elected not to adopt a new livery but simply rebranded their locomotives which still carried their previous liveries, this being for many the former Trainload freight triple grey. This applied mainly to Class 37, 56 and 60 locomotives. The elysian setting of Forder viaduct 'which crosses a creek off the Lynher river', can be photographed from the north west side during the mid-summer months.

USA RIO GRANDE AND UNION PACIFIC, MINIATURE

Above: Dobwalls Adventure Park, Saturday, 8 June 1996: Rio Grande 2-8-2 No. 498 *Otto Mears*. This is a model of K37 (No. 498), a three foot gauge prototype of the Denver and Rio Grande system.

The 7¼in (184 mm) gauge miniature railway network operated as part of the Dobwalls Adventure Park, a family run visitor attraction in the Cornish village of Dobwalls. It was founded in 1970 by John Southern OBE but was regrettably closed in autumn 2006. The precision scale models were a source of admiration by all the visitors who came to ride the themed lines with their semblance of a variety of aspects defined by the USA railroads portrayed by these marvellous miniatures.

Opposite above: Dobwalls Adventure Park, Saturday, 8 June 1996: Union Pacific DDA40X Do-Do number 6908 *Centennial* seen on the impressive turntable.

The miniature railway was based on two very different American railroad routes, the Rio Grande Cumbres Pass line and the Sherman Hill route of the Union Pacific Railroad; passengers experienced an authentic ride through tunnels, over bridges and trestles and into canyons.

VIRGIN TRAINS

Below: Powderham, Tuesday, 6 August 2002: Passing the Exe Estuary, Class 47/4, in Virgin Trains livery, is operating a Virgin CrossCountry service, the 08.40 Glasgow Central to Penzance.

Classic posters provided by the Southern Railway carried an image of a young girl looking up to a steam locomotive driver and saying she was taking an early holiday, 'cos I know summer comes soonest in the South'. Certainly, the crowds of holiday makers that travel down to the South West each summer expect weather similar to that seen here – although the guarantee of such is wildly ambitious. Whether the quality of travel was improved in the Voyager units that replaced these locomotive hauled carriages is very debatable – unless you like cramped seating with a view of the plastic seat in front of you.

WEST MIDLANDS RAILWAY

Worcester Viaduct and bridge, Wednesday, 27 March 2019: 3-car Class 170/6 'TurboStar' crosses with a late afternoon service from Birmingham New Street to Hereford.

West Midlands Railway is operated by West Midlands Trains as part of the West Midlands franchise. The Worcester railway viaduct, part of which is to be seen on the left, is 855m (935 yards) long, and has 68 arches. I preferred the previous London Midland livery of white, black and green that embellished the West Midlands Trains fleet when that company took over the franchise. This interim West Midlands Railway gold carried by the Class 170 diesel unit is certainly enhanced by the golds and yellows of the setting sun drawing out such hues as seen reflected in the tranquil waters of the River Severn and echoed off the tower of Worcester Cathedral in the background. This whole area was severely affected by flooding in February 2020.

Ledbury Viaduct, Saturday, 9 April 2022: 3-car Class 172 'TurboStar' crosses with the 15.50 Birmingham New Street to Hereford.

This Grade II listed red brick viaduct, built 1859-60 for the Worcester and Hereford Railway Co., with its impressive thirty round-headed arches on slender piers, is a reminder of the vast number of railway viaducts which cross valleys throughout the land. They perform a functional role, yet many of them are awe-inspiring testaments to the quality of work carried out by the proud railway engineers who constructed the lines along which they feature. Their lasting impression on the surrounding towns and countryside is such that they form an essential part of the very heart of the locations above which they stride. Each viaduct can enhance the appearance of the everyday train as it crosses, intertwined as each is with the other within the world of railway architecture. How lucky we are indeed to inherit such a treasure trove.

WEST YORKSHIRE PTE

Fitzwilliam, Tuesday, 9 April 1991: Class 307 307111 departs with the 15.41 Doncaster to Leeds service.
These electric multiple units were previously operated providing heavily used commuter services on the Great Eastern Main Line when working out of London Liverpool Street station. They were redeployed briefly, after withdrawal in 1991 by Network SouthEast, for use on the newly electrified 'Metro Train' service between Leeds and Doncaster via Wakefield. In this guise they survived in such use until 1993 when they were withdrawn, to be replaced by much more modern Class 321/9 electric multiple units which were built at York by BREL in 1991.

WELSH HIGHLAND RAILWAY

Aberglaslyn Pass, Welsh Highland Railway, Sunday, 30 May 2010: 7863 2-6-2 + 2-6-2T NG/G16, No. 138, ex-South African Railways, one of the last Garratts built by Beyer-Peacock, is seen travelling south along the Afon Glaslyn hauling the 12.10 Caernarfon to Beddgelert and Pont Croesor .

This magnificent locomotive entered service at Port Shepstone, on the south coast of South Africa, in 1958. After 1986, the locomotive was in active regular use as a shunter at the time it was withdrawn and shipped to the UK.

The Aberglaslyn Pass is one of the better known natural features that are traversed by the Welsh Highland Railway. The spectacular steep-sided valley enshrouds the river, the Afon Glaslyn, a powerful torrent draining the south side of Snowdon and the east side of Moel Hebog. Passing steam trains announce their presence as they echo off the sides of the valley and leave a lasting impression of sound and steam amidst such dramatic scenery. Passengers have been able to share this awesome pageant since this section of line reopened to passengers on 21 May 2009.

FINALE

Laira Depot, Sunday, 15 September 1991: Class 52 'Westerns' on display at the Depot Open Day. Preservation bases are given for the time of the photograph.

From left to right we see

D1035 *Western Yeoman*, ex-D1010 *Western Campaigner*, very recently based at the West Somerset Railway after having been in restoration at Didcot,

D1013 *Western Ranger* based at the Severn Valley Railway,

D1015 *Western Champion* based at Old Oak Common,

D1023 *Western Fusilier* on loan from the National Railway Museum and temporarily based at the South Devon Railway,

D1062 *Western Courier* based at the Severn Valley Railway.

Open Days such as this are usually linked to raising funds for a local or national charity. The intent is to draw a good crowd and for dry weather to favour the efforts of those who have laid on such a splendid collection of locomotives. The contrast in colours, exemplifying the variety of liveries worn by the 'Westerns', is particularly noteworthy and is a credit to the depot's managers who have managed to arrange this eye-catching parade. Local enthusiasts will have been particularly rewarded to see such an assemblage of locomotives from the same Class, which recalls the heyday of the Western Region diesel hydraulics. Many of the various workings over their traditional stamping ground within Devon and Cornwall have featured in countless railway books and magazines – a tribute indeed to the legacy which is honoured in this line-up.

Royal Albert Bridge, Wednesday, 23 March 2022: Class 66/0 66168 departs from the Royal Albert Bridge with the 14.32 Parkandillack to Exeter Riverside China Clay wagons.

  The fact that in modern times many of the UK's freight trains are in the capable hands of Class 66s in a small variety of liveries, hauling standardised bulk loads for a variety of clients, means that the kaleidoscope of colours seen on our modern railways is somewhat restricted and not at its most prolific. For the operators, such standardisation of traction means simpler maintenance and availability of spare parts, with less requirement for drivers to have knowledge of such a diverse range of locomotive types as in the past. Yet these same trains perform an important part in relieving the congested roads along which convoys of lorries, vans and private cars all compete for space, such as seen on the Tamar road bridge in the background of this picture, just before the evening rush hour peak. Freight transport routes form the arteries of modern economies. City dwellers expect a constant supply of fresh produce on supermarket shelves and rapid online shopping deliveries to their door. Just-in-time deliveries are crucial for companies enmeshed in ever more complex production networks. It can only be hoped that greater incentives to facilitate improved use of the rail network to move freight will be forthcoming, accompanying global moves towards reduced transport emissions linked to a cleaner and less polluted environment.

Birmingham Snow Hill, Saturday, 23 April 1988: Class 31/4 31413 *Severn Valley Railway* on display, named the previous day by Mr Sidney Newey, Director of Provincial Services for BR, at a ceremony at Bewdley station. On the left is Class 27 27059.

Distinctive with its light blue band and wrap around yellow cab ends, this livery variation may be a little too excessive in its assemblage of colours which some may have found too gaudy. Admittedly we live in an age where some locomotives operated by European national railways such as DB (German Railways) are embellished with full side adverts, and colourful adverts promoting regional cultural and historic visitor attractions in the UK have until recently featured on diesel multiple units. These can prove to be either distracting or enhancing otherwise plain liveries. The viewer is the target of such schemes and thus here with this Class 31, the travelling public and photographers will make their choice. It is intriguing that relatively few pictures of this Class 31 in the livery shown either feature on line or in specialist books about the Class, so we may conclude that it seems to have conveyed less appeal than presumably was hoped for.

Devonport Cutting, Thursday, 8 August 1991: a Class 47/4 passes with the 13.32 Penzance to Leeds parcels train.

With a mixed-colour rake of parcels carriages each wearing a different livery that would have been worn during the era recalled in this book, here is a scene which in terms of the railway traction and train formation has entirely changed – and in this case has also been lost to road competition. Whether it can be successfully argued that the current UK railscene is as colourful during this age of privatisation and changing franchises is, of course, a subjective decision and certainly there is a commendable variety of colour when compared to some of the nearest European nationalised railways' trains bearing standardised colour schemes. However, this passing parcels train is an image recalling an everyday event in the southwest now entirely relegated to the history books. Hopefully the fact that many books which are now being published recollect the impressive variety of locomotives and rolling stock with their characteristic liveries and heritage, which so forms a rich tapestry of Britain's railways past and present, pays adequate tribute to the sustained interest which this fascinating transport sector holds; long may it continue.

BIBLIOGRAPHY

BR Gradient Main Line Profiles, Ian Allan Publishing, 2003
CLARKE, D., *Diesels in Depth Class 40,* Ian Allan Ltd, 2006
COWARD, A., 'InterCity 125 High Speed Tribute', Mortons Media Group Ltd, 2021
HERRING, P., *Classic British Steam Locomotives*, Abbeydale Press, 2000
MARSDEN, C.J., *Foster Yeoman The Rail Story 75 years of aggregate by Rail*, Channel AV Publishing, 1998
MORRISON, Gavin, *British Railway DMUs in Colour*, Ian Allan Publishing, 2010